CONCILIUM

Religion in the Eighties

CONCILIUM

Editorial Directors

General Secretariat: Prins Bernhardstraat 2, 6521 AB Nijmegen, The Netherlands

Concilium 181 (5/1985): Sociology of Religion

CONCILIUM

List of Members

Advisory Committee: Sociology of Religion

YOUTH WITHOUT A FUTURE?

Edited by
John Coleman
and
Gregory Baum

English Language Editor
Marcus Lefébure

T. & T. CLARK LTD
Edinburgh

October 1985
T. & T. Clark Ltd, 36 George Street, Edinburgh EH2 2LQ
ISBN: 0 567 30061 X

ISSN: 0010-5236

Typeset by C. R. Barber & Partners (Highlands) Ltd, Fort William
Printed by Page Brothers (Norwich) Ltd

Concilium: Published February, April, June, August, October, December.
Subscriptions 1985: UK: £19.95 (including postage and packing); USA: US$40.00 (including air mail postage and packing); Canada: Canadian$50.00 (including air mail postage and packing); other countries: £19.95 (including postage and packing).

CONTENTS

Open Letter from the Theologians   ix

Editorial
JOHN COLEMAN
GREGORY BAUM   xiii

Part I
Youth Without a Future?

Can Youth be Defined?
RENÉ LAURENTIN   3

Contemporary Youth Movements in Europe and America:
An Overview
BARBARA HARGROVE   8

'Even a Good Education Gives Rise to Problems':
The Change in Authority between Parents and Children
PAUL KAPTEYN   19

Part II
The Economic Dimension

Unemployment and Young People in the Netherlands
KEES KWANT   37

An Analysis of Youth Unemployment and Future Prospects
for Jobs. The Case of Canada
AL HATTON   48

The Effect of Being out of Work on Young People in Chile
JUAN ANDRÉS PERETIATKOWICZ   57

Part III
The Meaning Dimension

Youth Malaise and Religion: The Case of Hungary
MIKLÓS TOMKA   65

'And so to bed': Protest and Malaise among Youth in
Great Britain
EILEEN BARKER   74

Part IV
The Apocalyptic Dimension

Young People and the Nuclear Threat
MICHAEL WARREN   83

Part V
Alternative Responses to a Hopeful Future

Youth in the World Council of Churches
ANS JOACHIM van der BENT   97

The Challenge of Youth: A New Prophetic Paradigm
JACQUES GRAND'MAISON   108

Contributors   119

Open Letter from the Theologians of *Concilium*

ABOUT THE FORTHCOMING SYNOD

TWENTY YEARS ago the Second Vatican Council made a considerable impact not only on the Roman Catholic community, which took on a new lease of faith and hope, but also on many other persons outside who learned to look at Roman Catholics with fresh sympathy. This anniversary year an Extraordinary Synod of bishops is due to study where the Church stands in relation to Vatican II. This Synod, however, will open in an atmosphere of hardening attitudes, weariness or even indifference.

The contrast between the impact of the Council and the atmosphere hanging over the Synod is a particularly disturbing sign for us theologians of the review *Concilium* since, as its very name implies, it was born out of and for the Council. We wonder whether the faithful at large realise the full significance of the Synod, whether they are not overlooking the potential this Synod has to be a vital follow-up to the Council, whether they are doing enough to help the bishops exercise their office as Vatican II defined it.

At the distance of twenty years we also realise that Vatican II was not free of a certain kind of optimism, even naivete—this was the mood of the sixties in the West. We know, too, that some of its positive initiatives have been checked, distorted, even set at nought by the obstinate resistance of various groups or pockets of bureaucracy, and by the intemperance of other groups or individuals.

Nevertheless, we call on all members of the Catholic Church not to forget the various ways in which the Council was able to make available anew so many riches of authentic Christian tradition and so to bring their faith, their hope and their charity to more vibrant life. The people of God found a new confidence in itself and in the Church precisely as God's people, making the Bible, the Eucharist and the variety of ministries their own again. New voices have been heard. Not only lay people but bishops themselves began to experience the exercise of authority in a new way. Christians awoke to a deeper sense of such essential realities of practice and belief as revelation, the people of God, the Church, the world itself as something to have hope and joy about: *Gaudium et spes!*

Two quite decisive consequences of the Council bear upon the forthcoming Synod and risk being disregarded:

1. It is not only the bishops who are summoned to or represented at the Synod and affected by it, it is all the memebers of the local churches. The bishops, after all, are invited as the pastors of their people.

2. The Synod is not the master and judge of the Council, but its servant, and must allow itself to be judged in that light.

We are, of course, well aware that the difference between the welcome given to the Council twenty years ago and the coolness felt in regard to the Synod today is due to the great changes that have occurred outside as well as inside the Catholic community.

Outside, new realities have come to light: the emergence of countries and cultures beyond Europe, of the world of the poor (with what they want of us, but also with what they have to give us), of the world of women; the displacement of the centre of gravity from the Atlantic to the Pacific; the new economic situation of the North Atlantic community as a result of the current crisis and unemployment; the uncertainty of these countries about their values and their traditional cultures; the uncertainty of young people facing the future.

Within the Catholic community many people are asking questions, especially about Vatican II and what followed it: Did we go too far, or not far enough? Has the positive potential been exploited or buried? Have the negative aspects been recognised or suppressed? Even the undeniable benefits of the Council have brought in their wake changes which have sometimes created new problems. More importantly still, the people of God is searching for a new awareness of itself as it tries to listen to voices from its midst which have until now been silent: the voices of the poor, of women; the voices of Africa, Latin America and Asia; the voices of the oppressed churches of East and West, North and South. As a result, the different local churches sometimes give the impression of hesitating between rigidity and weariness; between the restoration of a Church too old in a world too new and the inability to build up churches vital enough to cope with an impossible world. And while we wait, too many suffer on account of the lack of progress on problems as important for the people of God as ecumenism, the status of women in the church, the organisation of ministries, the leadership of base communities, the legitimate and traditional autonomy of religious orders.

In this situation, and bearing in mind what happened at recent synods, we wish to appeal to the faith and hope of all Catholics. We wish to communicate our conviction that the Spirit of Jesus Christ can blow through the Church, today in 1985 as it did at Vatican II, and as it has on so many occasions since the first Pentecost when it found a way to speak to every man and woman in each their own tongue. We want to share our hope that the next Synod can be good news for the world. And this is why we want to insist on at least two essential preconditions for the success of the Synod which we fear may be overlooked.

The first condition is that we all, individually and together, commit ourselves to help our bishops be true to their calling. This Synod will be the work, under the presidency of the Pope, of certain bishops, especially of the presidents of the episcopal conferences, elected by the bishops of their countries. These bishops can discharge their office only if we in our turn discharge ours, each according to our ability. This applies to us theologians in the service of Catholic communities and their bishops. It applies especially to all those who only too often have been rejected and to whom we (and the Synod) need to give back their say, even as Jesus did for the rejects of his time against the civil and religious authorities massed against Him.

It is not a question of helping our bishops to look back twenty years to see whether the Church has duly respected Vatican II. It is a question of helping our bishops to look twenty years ahead, to see how to build up tomorrow's churches in the light of Vatican II and in light of everything we have discovered together and the Spirit has disclosed to us since then.

A second condition for the success of the Synod depends directly on the bishops themselves. We recall with feeling and gratitude the power, freedom, faith and generosity so many bishops showed at Vatican II and how often they were the inspired servants of the people of God. We beg the bishops at the 1985 Synod to show the same resourcefulness, the same independence of judgment, the same courage, the same hope. We ask them to speak out in a way that is beholden to no one, but is theirs by right. We ask them to exercise without fear the responsibility that Vatican II recognised in those who preside in the churches. We ask them to embody the power, the originality and the tenderness with which the Spirit of God addresses every woman and man in each generation.

When John XXIII opened Vatican II, he said to the bishops of the time: 'Do not listen to the prophets of doom who announce disasters, as if the end of the world were at hand. . . . Everything, even human differences, leads to the greater good of the Church.' Today, before the opening of the Synod we bear in mind the words of Jesus Christ that John Paul II is fond of repeating, and we dare to say to the bishops: 'Do not be afraid.' Do not be afraid of the world that is ours today. Do not be afraid of the world to be built tomorrow. Do not be afraid of anything—in us and in yourselves—that tends to make you take refuge in the past or tarry in the shadows. Do not be afraid of anything that might trap us into merely repeating ourselves instead of releasing a new word. Today too, in 1985, with divine guidance and the unconquerable humility of Jesus Christ, the Spirit of God can do new things. Let us rise up, and go forth!

Editorial:
The International Year of Youth

THE UNITED Nations has declared 1985 the International Year of Youth. It proposes three main sub-themes for our reflections on the young during this current year: education, the fuller participation of youth in our societies, and peace. On its part, The European Youth Forum, a lobby-group in Brussels which plays an integral role within the European Economic community, notes that 40 per cent of those unemployed in the EEC countries fall in the age-range 15–25. It is determined to place the question of youth unemployment in the forefront of the European discussions during this International Year of Youth. Hundreds of unemployed European youth confronted their elected members at the European parliament in Strasburg last year in a protest project dubbed, 'Jobs Now'. Unfortunately, there simply does not yet exist a genuine European-wide plan to deal, systematically, with the issue of the growing and, perhaps, permanent situation of widespread youth unemployment.[1]

There lurks a great danger inherent in these United Nations' thematic years. Thus, in 1979 we celebrated the year of the child and, in other years, the year of the woman or the year of the handicapped. We court the temptation of restricting the significance of these thematic years to merely giving extra attention to various neglected groups, without paying sufficient heed to the perduring structural nature of their neglect and its impact on the quality of our societies. As Ad Malkert notes in respect to the Netherlands, 'In the end, the success of the Year of Youth will be measured by the answer to the question whether this year had as its result a greater involvement of youth in their own future and a concomitant shift in policy by the government'.[2]

1. YOUTH SEES ITS OWN FUTURE

Various sociological surveys in different industrial countries show that youth itself is not entirely certain about its own future. One Dutch survey indicates that half of those under 21 have difficulty imagining future optimal, or even successful, solutions to the issues of nuclear threat and ecological damage to the milieu.[3] Similarly, a poll conducted by the British newspaper, *The Observer*, found a majority of British teenagers, aged 15–18, concluding that Britain would be a worse place over the next twenty years, 'a more violent, careless, possibly dead society'. Pessimism rules. Nuclear war is considered the biggest cloud on the horizon. Attitudes to government are cynical. Significantly, unemployment represents the second major topic, after the nuclear threat, raised by this sample of British youth, seemingly uncertain about their own future.[4]

Reflecting on related comparative data for youth in the United States, the Harvard psychiatrist, John E. Mack, comments: 'As many American young people grow older, they become afraid that they may have nothing to look forward to. They are uncertain about making lasting commitments to a future that they doubt they will ever see. For one rock music group, The Sex Pistols, "no future", a line from one of their songs became virtually a motto.'[5]

Youth is such a rich and varied theme it would be almost impossible to do justice to the full range of the topic in one volume of *Concilium*. In preparing this volume, several of our consultants objected to putting a question mark behind the topic phrase. For them, as Jacques Grand'Maison states in his contribution to this volume, it is paradoxical to speak about youth without a future since the two terms seem naturally conjoined. The editors of this volume, however, have decided to stay with this paradoxical wording as a way of underscoring the evidence from the many sociological surveys which indicate that in the industrial lands a large body of youth itself presently questions its own future. Whatever the massive differences, in other respects, between East and West Europe, the two blocs exhibit comparatively large statistical increases over the past decade in youth alcoholism, drug use, suicides, criminality and a growing abstention from involvement in politics and the organisational life of society (labour unions, mediating associations, the churches).[6] These statistics would seem to indicate a crisis of meaning, what the great French sociologist, Emile Durkheim, called anomie.

We need not romanticise the young. We can state without hesitation, however, that youth represents a seismographic function in society, registering in their movements and aspirations economic, social and cultural ground-shifts. If contemporary youth is experiencing doubts, in new and sizable measures, about the meaning of their future, the same question mark hangs on the future of us all. It does absolutely no good to blame the cultural symptom recorders. As several contributions to this *Concilium* volume suggest, the cause for a failure in meaning—the current cultural crisis in advanced industrial societies—may lie more with the contemporary generation of adult leadership in our major societal institutions, including the churches, than with youth as such.

2. DEFINING YOUTH

In his contribution to this volume, René Laurentin wisely reminds us of the ambiguity and relativity inherent in the term, youth. Thus, for example, in the so-called fourth world in Western Europe (the 5 + per cent poorest who are members of a permanent sub-class) the period of youth is, often, totally over by age 18–20. Laurentin also recalls that the concept, youth, has important mythic dimensions.

We want to enter into this mythic dimension of youth for a moment. Psychologists tell us that succeeding generations, our own children or their surrogates in youthful successors, represent a species of objective, if provisional, immortality. If the future of our youth is placed in serious question, our own future lies in jeopardy as well. If they experience a crisis of meaning in the on-going project of our societies, then we face serious diminishment in our abilities to experience generativity and the creative summing up of a meaningful life in a contemplative wise old age. As the great psychologist, Erik Erickson has taught us, a serious crisis of meaning in any one sector of the life-cycle from birth to death provokes or points to a concomitant crisis in the other sectors.

3. THE ECONOMIC DIMENSION: UNEMPLOYMENT

The future of our youth confronts us with psychological questions. We have not neglected touching on the psychological dimension in this volume (see especially the contributions of Juan Peretiatkowicz, Paul Kapteyn and Jacques Grand'Maison). Nevertheless, the editors of this volume have decided, purposefully, to emphasise in a special way the economic and structural aspects of the youth problem, especially in connection with the issue of youth unemployment. Large scale and growing youth unemployment is a relatively new problem in Western Europe and the North Atlantic countries. Even some Eastern European countries (e.g. Yugoslavia with its current 1,000,000 unemployed) now face the same problem. Youth unemployment or under-employment has long been endemic in the urban areas in such third world countries as Peru, Bolivia and Chile. In his contribution, Jacques Grand' Maison reminds us that youth represents the majority of the world's population. But especially in third world countries youth represents, demographically the majority. In Western and Eastern Europe and the North Atlantic nations the demographic statistics register close to zero population growth and a serious greying of the population pyramid. We cannot pay special attention to contemporary youth without turning our eyes toward the third world.

We will find no easy fix to the problem of structural unemployment and its impact on youth in the first world. In a social analysis of the Canadian economy, Michael Czerny, SJ, and Jamie Swift comment: 'It has gradually dawned on people that the economy is not organised to provide jobs. Unemployment is not an aberration or a temporary faltering in an otherwise steady march of economic growth. It seems to be a chronic condition that worsens with each backward swing of the economic pendulum . . . The logic of private profit and corporate growth takes priority over job-creation . . . Before the eighties, when employment tailed off in one area of the economy, there always seemed to be a new opening for labour. The unemployment of the eighties, however, is qualitatively different from earlier downturns, recessions and depressions. Jobs are evaporating, with little prospect of broad new horizons opening up.'[7]

It seems to us that it would have represented a trivialisation of the International Year of Youth not to have essayed the topic of future employment opportunities for youth in the industrial nations and the third world. Various religious groups have already addressed this issue. The US Bishops' Conference in its in-process pastoral letter, 'Catholic Social Teaching and the US Economy', decries the high rates of unemployment tolerated in the United States. Cardinal Willebrands of the Netherlands wrote a pastoral letter just before his recent retirement pleading the cause of the youthful unemployed. The West German bishops have also addressed the issue of youthful unemployment.[8]

In their excellent pastoral letter, 'Ethical Reflections on the Economic Crisis', (1983) the Canadian Catholic bishops said the following about unemployment: 'By creating conditions for permanent unemployment, an increasingly large segment of the population is threatened with the loss of human dignity. In effect, there is a tendency for people to be treated as an impersonal force having little or no significance beyond their economic purpose in the system.'[9] For its part, the General Synod of the Anglican Church in Canada declared in 1978 that 'unemployment inflicts much greater harm on the poor than inflation does. The persistence of high rates of unemployment, year in and year out, is in fact an instrument of oppression, whether intended or not.'[10]

The articles by Kees Kwant, Al Hatton and Juan Peretiatkowicz in the second and central section of this volume demonstrate that youth are the first to suffer from the new permanent structural unemployment in the wake of the so-called third industrial revolution. Kwant argues that even for those in the Netherlands who obtain jobs, the spectre of future unemployment entails fear, caution and a certain conformity. Currently in the Netherlands, of those 18 years old or under, 30 per cent fewer enjoy employment than in 1979. In 1985, 100,000 Dutch young people completed a full year after their school leaving without obtaining any job. 15 per cent of the Dutch university graduates in 1984 have not succeeded in gaining employment.[11] Kwant provides us, in his article, with a general ideal-type scheme to categorise workers: motivated workers who enjoy their work intrinsically; dutiful workers who find no inner meaning in their work; those who are willing to work but without any great zest. Kwant fears that the third industrial revolution will increase permanent unemployment and decrease the number of jobs where work promises something mid-way between true creativity and pure mechanical labour.

Al Hatton, in his contribution, directs our imaginations to alternative forms of job creation and shared jobs. We wish to underscore two of the points he makes in this article. First, over and above the economic dimension of youth unemployment, other areas of economic short-sightedness involve a heavy borrowing against future generations. Thus, for example, in the United States serious, even radical, questions have been broached as to whether the social security and old age pension welfare arrangements presently operative will sustain the retirement of those currently under thirty years of age. Today's youth may not have their elder's welfare umbrella in the future. Similarly, servicing and retiring the extraordinary debt crisis in Latin American countries (especially Brazil, Argentina, Mexico and Venezuela) places a heavy financial burden and economic mortgage on those presently under age twenty-one in those lands.

Many studies of youth unemployment substantiate a second point made by Hatton (among others, the article in this volume by Juan Peretiatkowicz). As a rule, young people are unlikely to resort to social analysis. They do not see their unemployment in larger structural terms. They tend to individualise or psychologise the issue. Hence, they speak of the energetic vs. the lazy or blame themselves, if unemployed, or others, if employed. We can draw a lesson from this. We need, as a Church, to point out the importance of addressing the issue of youthful unemployment with the tools of social analysis as part of an integral youth apostolate which will prepare this generation of Church youth to see, judge and act for themselves on Christian values. Otherwise, our church youth work runs the risk of becoming an individualist ideology, a danger to which Michael Warren alerts us in his article.

We could have duplicated Peretiatkowicz' acute study of the effects of unemployment on Chilean youth for youth in Peru, Ecuador, Argentina and, especially, Bolivia. One of the editors of this issue, (John Coleman) spent the last two summers living with a middle-class Bolivian family in Cochabamba, Bolivia. The parents of this family want their two sons to emigrate to the

United States. Their laconic judgment states their understanding of Bolivian economic realities: 'There is no future for the youth in this country.' Peretiatkowicz also alerts us to the double corruption of youth involved in high levels of youthful unemployment. Youth unemployment drives the young to bodily and psychically destructive behaviour (drugs, alcohol, sexuality, crime) which will make it more difficult for them to built a secure future, even if or when the current crisis of neo-liberal economics in Chile has passed.

4. INTER-GENERATIONAL CONTACT

In the first section of this volume we open the discussion on youth with three over-view articles. René Laurentin alerts us to the problems of the definition of youth and proposes as a working definition, 'the time of transmission of culture and the human and ecclesial heritage'. Laurentin reminds us of the necessary dialectic between transmission of received wisdom and the search for the new. In this regard, we might have enriched this volume by the addition of articles which attended to youth life-styles and self-expression which lead to the setting apart or ghetto-isation of youth. The eighties do not exhibit much generational conflict. In social surveys the majority of youth in Europe and North America state that they get along well with their parents. This decade, however, also does not exhibit a great deal of inter-generational contact. In this regard, a recent study of Swedish youth notes the important desire of young people in Sweden for a genuine, humane and intimate contact with older adults.[12]

Barbara Hargrove's contribution explicitly relates the emergence of youth protest movements of the 1960s to altered perceptions of the culturally prevalent views of the future. She relates the post-World War II expectations of a new age of freedom, anti-authoritarianism and prosperity in Western Europe and North America and the concomitant hope for a new, more just, society in Eastern Europe. In both East and West, these post-war ideologies have long since spent their earlier vitalities. In the 60s and 70s post-war ideology yielded to utopia, what Laurentin refers to as 'living on dreams'. While the era of youthful protest and movement has now passed, the basic underlying structural and conjunctural causes which gave rise to that protest remain. For Hargrove, contemporary youth movements provide us with symptoms of a new cultural paradigm, a shift to post-industrial society. She deems this shift as momentous as the Reformation of the sixteenth century. Other authors are less sanguine. It should be noted, however, that Hargrove's analysis remains, in some respects, parochial. It does not attend to those continents where the over-whelming majority of today's youth live.

In a final contribution to this first, over-view, section, Paul Kapteyn, relying primarily on Dutch evidence, suggests that some of the statistical evidence for growing youth crime in Western countries may be less negative than it, at first glance, appears. Kapteyn reminds us of the fact that the increase in youth criminality pre-dates the rise in youth unemployment. It has an independent cause. Kapteyn locates his causal explanation of the phenomenon in a shift in authority structures. Using the example of the school system, he maintains that a sharp decrease in hierarchical authority patterns typifies contemporary educational structures in the west. Direct, heteronomous control systems yield to discipline based on self-control. Kapteyn's article represents our explicit attempt, in this volume, to touch base with one of the sub-themes of the United Nations Year of Youth, education.

We presume that the widespread evidence of a decline, in the industrial lands, of the generation gap and inter-generational conflict reflects parallel shifts in patterns of exercising authority within the family system. Here, too, we can speak of a less hierarchical, authoritarian and heteronomous exercise of authority. Kapteyn notes, in relation to educational systems, that, more than formerly, good classroom order must base itself on mutual respect and trust. Family authority between parents and children seems to have undergone similar shifts. Thus, recent surveys of Dutch and West German adolescents show 90 per cent of the Dutch youth (70 per cent in West Germany) responding that they get along very well with their parents. They also show that, compared to a decade ago, youth who live at home are more likely to determine for themselves when, where and for how long they leave their parents' house for entertainment or dates, a sign of greater youth autonomy.[13] Perhaps, one reason for that widespread aversion to contemporary religious institutions and ideologies in the West noted by Hargrove lies in the fact that the churches have not undergone parallel shifts in their mode of exercising authority. Their more hierarchical, heteronomous exercise of authority finds itself out of kilter with the prevailing cultural model. Whatever the explanation, the churches in the first world seem especially hard hit by youth apathy, dis-engagement and alienation. We will return to this point a little further on.

5. SIGNS OF ANOMIE

The third section of this volume addresses the meaning dimension as this affects contemporary youth's sense of the future. For reasons of space, we have had to limit our treatment of this theme to only two contributions, one from Eastern Europe and the second from Western Europe. Miklos Tomka writes about the situation of youth in Hungary. His contribution suggests that in Hungary economic conditions unduly prolong the period of adolescent dependence. Hungarian youth find it very difficult, until their mid-thirties, to fulfil two of the three conditions Tomka postulates for adult independence: a place in society's work-structure; independent living arrangements; and a bonded, sexual and/or affectional relationship. Tomka, however, signals for Hungary a more general Eastern European phenomenon: a current religious revival among youth. East Germany, Yugoslavia and Slovakia have also experienced this revival, much to the chagrin of the authorities.

In the Hungarian situation, however, the youth see the institutional Church as formal, distant, a liturgy without a community. As other commentators on the religious situation in Hungary have noted, the future of the church lies in the basis-groups so attractive to the young. These provide a sense of genuine community, a safe haven for greater consciousness and a break with isolationism. Unfortunately, however, the Hungarian hierarchy seems dead-set against the basis-group movement in its midst. Paradoxically, Hungary's authorities chide their youth for the same meaningless consumers' mentality and individualism for which Western youth, in its turn, is often indicted. We will be misled if we restrict our judgment of youth to this sort of moralism.

Eileen Barker's companion piece to Tomka's about malaise and meaninglessness among English youth alerts us to important differences in England between working-class youth movements and those of the middle class. Barker also underlines the importance of youth unemployment as a key variable to understand the crisis of meaning among British youth. Protest has yielded to apathy. In the modern welfare State, absolute poverty has been abolished. But the State does not provide an opportunity for its youthful members to contribute to the on-going meaning and renewal of society's project. Barker touches base, in this contention, with the second sub-theme of the UN International Year of Youth, participation. Hungary and Britain present paradoxical, comparisons. In the former country, the Kadar government's unspoken social contract depends, for regime legitimacy, on Kadar delivering on economic welfare. The economic crisis robs this pact—and the society it founds—of its fundamental meanings. Western welfare capitalism rests, at base, on a similar contract. Both authors complain that in their respective countries there is diminished opportunity for youth to participate in the society's projects.

6. YOUTH AND PEACE

Peace is the third sub-theme for this UN Year of Youth. Michael Warren's article, basing its conclusions largely on North American evidence, addresses the impact of the nuclear threat on young people. Warren stresses in his contribution the necessary inter-connection between the generations. Young people, he maintains, do not shrink from contact with adults who communicate that life and human values are worth fighting for. Warren notes the rising suicide rate among youth in the United States, a statistic reduplicated in almost every Western European and some of the Eastern European countries (e.g. especially Hungary). He warns against youthful revivals in the Church based on cheap grace, renewal programmes or spiritual movements which lack the perceptual courage to face social, structural problems of long-range duration. Warren pleads for a renewed Church ministry to youth based on solidarity with victims, non-violence and a spirituality of resistence. He turns our attention, again, to the place where the majority of the world's youth live, the third world.

7. YOUTH: A CHALLENGE TO THE CHURCH

The final two articles in this volume address the question of an appropriate Church response to the challenge of contemporary youth. In this regard, we find the sociological statistics, especially in Western Europe, concerning youth and the Church quite troubling. The decline in Church practice among Catholics, especially the young, in Belgium, for example, is so startling that the Belgium bishops, for the past several years, have simply refused to allow these statistics to be made public!

The Spanish journal, *Religion y Cultura*, devoted a recent special thematic issue to the International Year of Youth. In the lead article, entitled, 'Spanish Youth face to face with Religion', Isaias Diez del Rio notes that in Spain, 'youth and the Church represent two totally separate worlds, far from each other'. Is this distantiation, he asks, due to the fact 'that the Church and its present structures lack an appeal and convocational capacity vis-a-vis youth?'[14] Citing a range of Spanish sociological studies, Diez del Rio documents a steep—even vertiginous—decline in Church practice among young Spanish Catholics. Even in their self-descriptions, a growing number of Spanish young Catholics choose to identify themselves as ex-Catholics. Similar data exists for the Netherlands, Belgium, West Germany and Australia.[15] Diez del Rio wonders aloud if the Church is really doing very much to address this problem of a precipitous decline of youthful adherence to the institutional church. 'Is the Church really doing anything in this international year of youth?'[16]

Pastor van der Bent, in his essay in this volume, reviews the history of efforts within the World Council of Church's division on youth to address, over the years, the three themes of this UN Year of Youth: education, peace and participation. He rightly warns us against idolising youth. 'It is not youth which is the hope of the future but the future which is the hope of youth.' Van der Bent's historical over-view stresses the various ways the World Council of Churches attempts to give its youthful members full vote, participative voice and partnership in programmes and policies of their churches.

Originally, the editors sought to commission an essay which would parallel, for the international Catholic Church, van der Bent's historical over-view of the World Council of Church's efforts for youth. It did not prove possible, however, to engage a suitable author. Moreover, in retrospect, it became obvious that in a gerontocracy such as the Roman Catholic hierarchical system, even if we allow, following Laurentin, for the relativity of the concept of youth, few genuinely young men (and no women of any age) have active voice, creative partnership or genuine participation in setting pastoral guidelines or policy direction within the institutional church. There is no space within the decision-making organs of the Church for the true voice of youth. In the Catholic case, one must look to para-institutional movements such as, for example, the peace movement, the Focolari, the Catholic Worker Movement and other non-official spiritual and cultural movements of Catholics (including the base-groups in Latin America) to find the faces and engagement of young Catholics. As an institution, at present, the Roman Catholic Church lacks a young face.

For this reason, Jacques Grand'Maison's final, theological essay points to certain new directions needed for an evangelically grounded youth pastorate among Catholics in the industrial nations. Whether youth actually carries, in its movements and attitudes, the encapsulated future can remain for us a question of mythic thinking. Nevertheless, in fact a large number of pastors and parents, especially in Western Europe, in the absence of a strong youthful ecclesial representation, begin to question seriously whether the Church has a genuine future in their lands? This volume of *Concilium* suggests that the answer to these agonising questions depends on our answers to the prior questions of this volume: Does our youth have a future? How do we explain, wrestle with and, finally, change the economic, military and ideological threats to the future and sense of hope for our youth? We repeat. In addressing the future of youth, we broach our own futures. The Church called to function as the herald of the future, ever-renewed and renewing, always-coming and yet already-here, Kingdom of God can not let this International Year of Youth pass without serious reflection on its own relation to contemporary youth and its future.

We end with an image and a question. One of the editors of this volume (John Coleman) lives, this year, in the Belgium university town of Leuven. In the centre of the city stands a statue of a playful youth dubbed *Fonske*. The name represents the diminutive form of *Fons* taken from the Latin motto of the Catholic University of Leuven, *Fons Sapientiae* (seat of wisdom). The statue suggests that wisdom depends on a youthful spirit, contact with the ever young and young-making spirit of God. Without youth, it suggests, we find no renewal, no genuine perduring wisdom, no life-giving spirit. In this year of an extraordinary Synod of bishops to review the twenty years of international church life since Vatican Council II, we pose the following question: Would it not be appropriate for the bishops, in reviewing the consequences of the Council, to take as a hermeneutical horizon for their judgment, the impact of the Council on the world's youth? Such a hermeneutical horizon suggests less the need for a reactionary response of restoration than a deeper, more critical continuation of the energies of renewal unleashed by the Council. More boldly, would the bishops dare to invite young Christians as observers with voice at such a synod? Will the Church in its synod during this International Year of Youth dare to show a young face to the world or will it be a body busy, in the words of the Latin poet, Horace, with the business of being *laudator temporis acti*, full of praise for times long since passed?

JOHN COLEMAN
GREGORY BAUM

Notes

1. See Maurice van Lieshout 'Jongeren en de Europese Gemeenschap' in *Jeugd en Samenleving* 14, 5 (May 1984) 304–317.
2. Cited in Harro van Zijl 'Het International Jongerenjaar in Nederland' in *Jeugd en Samenleving* 14, 12 (December 1984) 789.
3. Hans van Ewijk 'De Jongeren' *Jeugd en Samenleving* 15, 2 (February 1985) 310.
4. See *The Observer*, magazine insert, Sunday 24 February 1985 p. 16.
5. John E. Mack 'Look Inside, Look Outside: Nuclear Winter is Here' in *The International Herald Tribune*, 3 March 1985 p. 8.
6. For comparisons between East and West Europe on these issues see Peter van der Zant 'Jeugdbeleid te star voor Jongeren' in *Jeugd en Samenleving* 14, 3 (March 1984) pp. 131–143.
7. Michael Czerney SJ and Jamie Swift *Getting Started: On Social Analysis in Canada* (Toronto 1984) pp. 73–74.
8. For Cardinal Willebrands' letter, see *Archief van de Kerken*, 39 no. 4 (April 1984) pp. 17–21. The West German bishops' letter is found in *Archief van de Kerken*, 38, no. 2 (February 1983) pp. 22–24.
9. Cited in Czerny and Swift, the work cited in note 7, p. 74.

10. Cited in Czerny and Swift, the work cited in note 7, p 73.

11. For these statistics, see Hans van Ewijk 'De Jongeren' the article cited in note 3.

12. *Ibid.*, p. 306.

13. *Ibid.*, p. 308.

14. See Isaias Diez del Rio 'La Juventud espanola ante la religion' *Religion y Cultura*, 30, 143 (November–December 1984) 627.

15. For Australia, see Graham Rossiter CFC. 'Why are Young Catholics not going to Mass' *The Australian Catholic Record*, 61, 1, 18–25.

16. Diez del Rio, *ibid.*, p. 631.

PART I

Youth Without a Future?

René Laurentin

Can Youth be Defined?

AN ISSUE devoted to youth must first define the notion of youth—mythical and relative though it is.[1]

1. A MYTHICAL NOTION

Mythical, because the word evokes values often to the fore in human discourse: youth is 'the future'; we need 'youthfulness' or a 'spirit of youth' in our institutions, etc. But organised or gerontocratic societies fear youth. Press headlines bear constant witness to this, especially recently. Young people have long been seen as lively, threatening, even aggressive. Bossuet, no less, evoked this fear provoked by the rising tide of youth: Hold back, he told them, 'Your turn will come soon enough'. This illustrates the fact that the rise of youth fans the fear of death felt by every human being: a tiresome disturbance. The myth has been well defined in terms of beginning and end, birth and death: myths evoke lost paradises and future paradises, in both the earthly and the heavenly meanings of these expressions. On the scientific level, these are the hypotheses of the initial 'big bang' and final cataclysm. Any discussion of 'youth' should be conscious of the mythology that tempts it and threatens it.

2. A RELATIVE NOTION

Youth is also a *relative* notion. In all families, the last-born are called 'the young ones', often till they die: 'The youngest of the family died first. He was only sixty', is the sort of thing I have often heard from the older siblings of

3

large families. Old workers become the young inmates of retirement homes, or the younger members of groups of pensioners.

So, how should we define youth? Not by a simple mathematical spread of age: from birth to 12, 15 or 30 years old; or else (distinguishing 'childhood' from 'youth') from 12 to 15—or even 40. This spread would vary too much from group to group and society to society.

3. NON-VIABLE DEFINITIONS

Neither can youth be defined as a proportion: the younger half, youngest third or quarter of the population. This would not fit either social perceptions, or the usual use of the word. It would also obfuscate discussion. Nor can it be defined by the health or dynamism which usually characterise youth. Illness and death affect all age levels, and there are apathetic young people just as there are some who bubble over with vitality. It is a remarkable fact that many old people keep the optimism, openness, passion and inventiveness that are usually supposed to belong to youth. This edifying staying-power is one of the finest characteristics of Christian holiness. John XXIII showed an admirable youthfulness of heart and spirit, capable of facing the risks posed by a different future, at the age of over seventy-seven. The Holy Spirit maintains the youth of the Church and Tradition, rejuvenating 'the very vessel which contains Tradition', as St Irenaeus said. The source of this phenomenon can be found in the eternal youth of God. But this theological notion, however interesting it might be, cannot serve as the basis for an overall definition.

4. A HANDING-ON PERIOD

Youth needs to be defined *according to its inherent relativity*, as we have seen, and stripped of the mythologies which cloud scientific study of the concept. The only sociological possibility is to define youth as *the time during which the human patrimony is handed on*. This manages to encompass the disconcerting evolutions of the word, and the variations in its application.

5. THE IMPACT OF EVOLUTION

The duration of youth varies with the time taken to hand on knowledge. In primitive, traditional societies, this handing-on process could be completed by the age of about twelve: the age of initiation. For cave man, it was probably even earlier. In our societies, with their overload of inheritance and memory, the time needed is prolonged to the age of 30, or even 40. This aspect is further complicated in the most advanced fields of scientific knowledge. Doctors and the like are competing and searching for a final position till somewhere around forty. This prolongation is not without its advantages: people often continue learning while they are also beginning to teach, and the dividing-line between the end of the learning period and the beginning of the period for research becomes harder to place in that scientists are always seeking for fresh knowledge. In the end, perhaps our societies will identify 'youth' with the whole of active life, after which a series of subtle, complex and sometimes draconian rules push those of retiring age into the ranks of the inactive population. But those who retire early (often against their will, and at under sixty) often show youthful qualities in their age group, which does not necessarily spell the end of creativity.

Other articles will look at the change that has taken place in youth, in the ever-accelerating process of change that is taking place in our society, in which 'on-going training' tends to prolong youth as capacity for learning, receiving, creating, as the development essential to the societies and groups of our times, which cannot survive without creating new things. It would seem that the classic definition of youth as the time taken to hand on knowledge (at the end of which one becomes active, responsible and productive) has been shattered by the flight into the future, which forces people to change ever more quickly if they are to remain competitive, and so survive. This change requires serious consideration.

6. YOUTH IN THE CHURCH

How does our definition apply to the Church? Easily, at first glance.

Youth is the time of *catechesis*, which hands on faith (knowledge and practice), and forms Christians to the point where they make their profession of faith, generally set at about the age of initiation in primitive societies: around the age of twelve.

The definition of youth is also easily applied in seminaries. There training leads to ordination, which gives qualifications, responsibilities and powers in the Church. The 'profession' (or consecration) equally shapes the curriculum in religious Orders or families. But youth is tending to be prolonged by the continued training and new starts which have become necessary in the Church as much as outside it.

Social evolution has further modified the age for the profession of faith or first communion (around twelve before Pius X, later in many Protestant communities), or solemn communion, which some people would like to see replaced by Confirmation. The problems this structure brings have become more acute since the beginning of the present century. In France, and elsewhere, the culmination of the process of initiation at around twelve often marks the end of religious practice and active life in the Church. Youth, which should normally lead to integration, effectiveness, responsibility, often leads to nothingness. This crisis in the handing-on of faith and this paradox are still among the major problems facing many churches.

7. HANDING-ON AND SEARCHING

The other problem is the articulation between the *handing-on* process which defines youth, and the process of *research* which has taken on such prominence in our civilisation that it ultimately threatens the whole concept of society, as well as that of youth. So the problem of youth and its definition leads on to a more generalised problem which is far from solution and needs to be constantly borne in mind.

Societies have long lived on their roots, their tradition, their repetitiveness. Today they tend to seek for their lives in the future, through a flight forwards. Some people would even oppose the *origin-God* of Tradition to the *future-God* of Progress. And this brings risks of disintegration. These risks have been taken more seriously over the past decade. One of the first signs of this was the formation of the 'Club of Rome', which turned its back on the one-sided view of Progress and recommended 'zero growth'. The rise of ecology, in which young people are prominently involved, points in the same direction.

8. TRADITION AND PROGRESS

The time the future was defined by progress, seen as an absolute value, seems to be past. The new problems posed by the future call for a better integration of the 'palaeo-cephalus' (the old brain) with the 'neo-cephalus' (the developments of the new brain). Human evolution cannot be a passage to heterogeneity: it develops the *new* on the basis of the *old*. The cerebellum and the palaeo-cephalus subsist under the developments of the neo-cephalus. This is written into man's biological make-up, not without consequences on the levels of his psychic and social life. Desiring and loving, being born and dying, learning for life, are part of this permanent process. And the cycle of renewal of society through the family perpetuates a world in which youth ends in men and women acceding to responsibility in becoming fathers and mothers, and becoming teachers in their turn.

In the Church, the classic notion of youth still has the importance inherent in Tradition, which forms the Church. *Tradition* means homogenous *handing-on* of essentials. It is vital. The question is how this handing-on, which defines youth, can be fitted in with the demands of a future which shows unprecedented openings: in accordance with the requirements for continued quest and the changes which John XXIII, who was still a traditionalist, moderately reinstated in the Church (under the name of *aggiornamento*)? How can the demands of research be taken into the future of the human race—and the future of God in the human race—without causing chaos? How then to allocate priorities between continuance and renewal, between evaluating and calling into question, the positive and the negative aspects of criticism (that is, of discernment): such are the questions this multi-disciplinary issue on youth can shed light on.

The process of handing-on human heritage, and the heritage of the Church has suffered violence and change. 'Youth' dreamed and exploded in revolutionary fashion in 1968. It has not stopped dreaming, but now sees more clearly that the dream does not include solutions.

Translated by Paul Burns

Note

1. Dictionary definitions tend to support the ambiguity of the term: 'Being young, adolescence, (the vigour or enthusiasm or weakness or inexperience or other characteristic of) the period between childhood and full manhood or womanhood' (COD); '1. the condition of being young, or youngness. 2. the appearance, freshness, vigour, spirit, etc., characteristic of one that is young. 3. the time of being young; early life. 4. the period of life from puberty to the attainment of full growth, adolescence . . .' (Hamlyn Encyc.).

Barbara Hargrove

Contemporary Youth Movements in Europe and America: An Overview

WHILE THERE are those who point to psychological dynamics to say that protest movements are endemic among youth, few would argue the point that they reached a particularly high point of intensity in the late 1960s. Any discussion of such movements from the vantage point of the mid-1980s must still take that period of ferment as its reference point, for current activism and withdrawal among youth depend in some measure upon that history.

'The Movement', which become the point of comparison for contemporary youth activity, includes in particular the campus disorders in the United States that began with the Berkeley Free Speech Movement in 1964 and effectively ended with the Kent State killings in 1970, the student uprisings in Frankfurt and the Free University of Berlin in 1967 and 1968, and in 1968 the 'revolutionary May' in Nanterre and Paris, the Italian and the Warsaw uprisings. These, of course, were only the areas of greatest intensity of a worldwide series of disorders among the young, in other areas of the countries mentioned and in many other nations as well. They also include a continuing phenomenon that has not received the attention of many movement specialists because it lies outside the realm of political protest, the youth counterculture that united young people around the world into a self-conscious social category in opposition to much of the culture of the cult of modernisation that lies behind most of the political and economic activity of the current world order.

To understand what is going on at the present time, it is important to look back to the period of those celebrated revolts, to see their underlying

8

assumptions and motivations. Some conditions that led to the more visible protests may have changed; many have not. Current youth responses to the world are directed both to the realities of the present situation and to perceptions that were forged in the earlier period.

Youth movements can be expected to arise out of certain preceptions of the future, since the period of youth is ordinarily defined as a time of preparation for adult roles, a time of decision-making that is expected to lead to commitments to a particular personal future in some given social nexus. Problems with the view of the future that were sources of the movements of the 1960s, of the breakdown in that process of decision-making, have not disappeared, yet the kind of ferment that swept college and university campuses and extended to other enclaves of youth in the late 1960s now seems muted. It is necessary, then, to try to explain both the rise and the diminution of youth movements in our time.

There is little doubt that typical intergenerational dynamics have contributed to contemporary youth movements. Any analysis of leaders and members of those protest groups will show a significant number whose actions and rhetoric indicate a strong desire to strike out at father-figures, a need to assert individuality, to claim one's own place. But in the 1960s there were at least three other forces working to create a climate that would support a general social movement: The international political situation, economic structures, and modern mass communications.

1. POLITICAL FORCES

World War II was acclaimed to have resulted in the defeat of authoritarian oppression, and to herald the dawn of a new age of freedom and prosperity. In the United States this euphoric nation was compounded by the rise of the nation to a position of international dominance, and it became the mood in which the first generation of children born after the war were raised. It was deliberately taught to West German youth through the denazification and reeducation programmes imposed upon that country in the immediate postwar years. American influence tended to link this confident view of the future to the American myth that on the North American continent a new society could be built that would transcend the aging traditions of Europe, lighting the way to a worldwide future of democratic freedom, justice, and equality. In Britain and countries of Western Europe other than Germany, the hope for the future was not tied so closely to the American model, but the expectation of a 'free world' was part of the milieu in which the post-war generation grew up.

Youth as Symptom

In Eastern Europe, particularly in Russia, the defeat of Hitler's Germany and the rise of the USSR to dominance had a similar stimulating effect on the young. Steeped in Marxist teaching that the dialectic of history was bringing their political forms to dominance, they worked at rebuilding a nation that could rival the American power that seemed to them to represent an outmoded bourgeois culture. Other Eastern European nations, less willing to allow their particularity to be absorbed by Russian power found among their young people many recruits for actions of resistance, but many others assumed the Russian pattern to be the wave of the future.

The first political movements that mobilised the young internationally after World War II were those concerned with the very real threat to the future of nuclear warfare, and the development of a balance of terror between the two 'superpowers'. Again, it was not youth alone who were involved in these movements, but it was in the anti-nuclear movement that there first emerged some of the alienation between the generations that dominated the 1960s and seems in large measure to be present in contemporary society. Given the destructive potential of atomic weaponry and its likelihood of killing women and children in greater numbers than military men, it became easier for youth to believe that the older generation was willing to sacrifice its children on the altar of national power.

In the West, precipitating political factors for the movements of the 1960s, each of which undermined the myth of American moral superiority, were the rise of the civil rights movement in the United States and the Viet Nam war. The civil rights movement aired the reality of inequality and injustice in the US, and cast doubts upon its ability to lead the world into a positive future. It provided experience in civil disobedience to many youth who were destined to become leaders in later movements, and it provided an ideology of nonviolence that was to be important in early stages of the youth revolt. This principle became one of the organising forces of the youth movement, according to Kenneth Keniston, who wrote in the mid-1960s that non-violence was a particularly necessary ideology for youth; whose inclusive and international understanding of themselves had to take violence and warfare as the primary enemy.[1] Although the principle of non-violence was, and continues to be, violated by youth movements, even their violent activity has been a striking out against other violence. At the beginning, non-violence was part of the hopefulness of the movement, for the effectiveness of non-violent tactics in the civil rights movement caught the attention of early youth movement leaders in the US.

By the early 1960s, young Blacks became engaged in 'sit-ins' to integrate racially segregated lunch counters in the American South, and young whites from the North volunteered to register voters and participate in 'freedom rides' and demonstrations where they learned the techniques of non-violence as well as the sense of community derived from common experiences of resistance. The first major outbreak on US campuses occurred at the University of California in Berkeley, led by Mario Savio, who was one of those who had experienced the civil rights movement when he volunteered to work in Mississippi for a summer. Observers such as Milton Viorst have stated that without the civil rights movement, the American youth movement would probably never have developed.[2]

The other precipitating incident in the West was the Viet Nam war. Here the US, proclaimed by itself and its allies as the friend of the weak, the champion of democracy, came to be seen as an international bully, exerting its power on a tiny and economically backward nation far from any territory it could claim to be protecting. To American youth this war offered particular proof of the nation's willingness to allow its young people to be killed for the sake of some kind of power game they could not comprehend, and American campuses were swelled by numbers of young men using college enrolment as a means of avoiding being drafted for the war. For European youth, particularly those in Germany who had been so carefully taught the difference between peaceloving, democratic America and Hitler's war machine, this was a betrayal of their newly adopted values. If this was the best that the best nation had to offer, where was the hope of the future?

In other countries of Western Europe there was a stronger tradition of political activity among students, so that political incidents, though important to them, were not as shattering to their usual view of the world. French students had been strongly supportive of the Algerian rebellion, and had already been aware of the Viet Nam situation because of the early French involvement there, so while disgusted with the 'dirty little war' being fought there by the US, they did not engage the issue as much from a position of disillusionment as did the American and West German students. Canadian youth were involved not only because of their ambivalent feelings toward their dominant neighbour to the south, but also because of the growing number of US emigrés to Canada who were avoiding military service, and who were involved with the Canadian young people as a matter of proximity if nothing else.

A parallel situation existed in Eastern Europe, where youth had cause to question the righteousness of the Marxist approach as they witnessed Russian repression of nationalist movements that claimed a socialist economy but sought their own interpretation of it. In both East and West, the notion of ideologies supported by military power undermined the hold those ideologies had on young minds.

2. ECONOMIC AND SOCIAL FACTORS

For many youth, from Blacks in the United States to French and Italian students, the precipitating factors of the movements of the 1960s were more economic and social than political. They were faced with a growing perception that university degrees did not necessarily result in employment of the sort they had envisioned, and in fact might end not just in lower status than they had hoped, but in actual unemployment. World War II had been an economic watershed, particularly for the more economically advanced nations of Europe and America, a time of movement beyond basic industrialisation to new levels of technology and of economic organisation. The rise of sophisticated technology demanded training at the levels of higher education for an increasing percentage of youth, but found the universities, and to some extent, the societies, unprepared to provide socialisation into the realities of the economic structure into which they were moving. Higher education, particularly in Europe, has been a rather élite enterprise. University training was expected to provide the skills and graces by which an élite might role and guide the society. In America, where technical and practical higher education has had a longer history, there still was the hope of high status associated with professional and technical expertise. At the very least, it was understood that the person who had completed a higher degree would be an independent actor in the economic structure, in command of a business or an area of expertise over which personal decision-making would exercise primary influence.

However, the complexities of the modern economy have required equally complex forms of organisation, in which individuals who may be very highly trained remain subject to decision-making at ever more distant levels, so that many university graduates have found themselves facing the same sorts of alienation of labour proclaimed by Marx as the fate of those who worked on factory assembly lines. This is the sort of 'proletarianisation of intellectuals' discussed by a number of current Marxian theorists. In addition, the sheer numbers of young people seeking higher education strained the capacities of the universities, turning them into the kind of impersonal bureaucracies that seemed to embody all the negative aspects of future setting for employment. Thus the future for which many university students thought they had been preparing themselves seemed torn from their grasp, and their years of preparation made meaningless.

Even more serious was the situation in some countries, particularly France and Italy, where the growth in university enrolment was not accompanied by growth in the number of jobs for university graduates. Unemployed graduates, or those who were underemployed, gave and continue to give the lie to those who advise university studies as the route to economic and social betterment. In America, much of the unrest of Black youth lay in the knowledge that many positions were not open to them, no matter how much training they may have had, and the same thing has held true in the attitudes of French Canadian youth and those of Northern Ireland.

3. MASS MEDIA AND THE RISE OF THE COUNTERCULTURE

Along with such objective conditions, there were also subjective sources of alienation and rebellion. Chief among them was the ascetic ideal of delaying gratification of personal desires during ever longer periods of training, in the midst (particularly in the West) of a 'consumer society' that sought more and more customers for its products. Similarly, forms of emotional management required by an industrial economy came more and more into question as young people learned Freudian arguments against repression. These 'cultural contradictions of capitalism'[3] led to a cultural revolt that has both set off youth as a generation apart and penetrated into the adult culture. Young people turned to, and in many ways, usurped, the bohemian world of the cultural élites. As Cyril Levitt has put it, 'Just as Luther had turned the world into a monastery, so did the counterculture turn the world of middle class youth into bohemia. Bohemia had come out of the closet.'[4]

There was also a self-consciousness, almost a self-righteousness, about this new youth culture, stimulated by the assumption of some of their mentors that only the young had the key to the future. In a period of rapid social change, adults could be compared to immigrants into a new society, where only the young were native-born.[5] While not all youth were so deliberate about it, some of their leaders sought to create in miniature their version of a worldwide utopian future, characterised by freedom, openness, love, and expressiveness.

Sources of international contact and the stimulation of discontent often came through these creative countercultural channels, particularly in the form of music. In the 1950s rock and roll was epitomised in the person of Elvis Presley, whose southern and lower class style helped youth to identify themselves as marginal to the middle class world which dominated their lives, as did the movie *persona* of the ill-fated James Dean. It was the Beatles, out of a working class English neighbourhood, who came to reign over an international culture of electronic music, which protested in both words and sound the rational order of modern society. They were followed by a host of media stars who created a musical milieu generally impenetrable by the adult generation. Psychedelic drugs offered new visions of reality, and young people began to 'tune-in, turn on, and drop out'. Many left home, moving to urban centres that were often near universities, where they joined one another in communal 'pads' where they attempted to live without the institutional structures they had come to abhor.

All of this made colourful footage for the television cameras, as did the rhetoric and violence attached to the political rebellions. Thus through the agency of the media, which had first dramatised the social problems to which the young were reacting, the movement became self-generating. The world of youth came to be a thing apart, set in opposition to the adult world. And while the majority of young people may never have become actively involved in any of these processes, it was this world of opposition to which they turned for a sense of identity.

The political consequences of this alternative culture were largely negative, for the more youth were identified as a group unto themselves, the less they were able to mobilise other social categories to join them in their protest. Student syndicalism grew as a movement dedicated to addressing the power structure of the university rather than wider issues, and while students were inclined to want to identify with Third World people as those who suffered from oppression similar to their own, there was a kind of élitism in the student ranks that made that identity suspect.

4. IDEOLOGY AND UTOPIA IN THE 1960s AND 1970s

Gianni Statera has made a good case for the idea that the early and formative youth movements in the 1960s were, in Karl Mannheim's terms, utopian. That is, their vision was total. They sought, not to reform the structures of society, but to tear down the old order so that a new one could take its place, even if it had not yet been formulated. The mood was not that of vicious destructiveness, but rather one of hope. This was particularly evident in the phenomenon of the French revolutionary May, when the enthusiasm of the young infected other social categories and came near to creating a full-scale revolution. The appeal and the weakness of such a utopian uprising can clearly be seen in these comments:

Indeed, as one of the most popular slogans of the Paris May says, it was imagination which seized power: and imagination built up a short-lived antisociety; it was unable to undermine or shape anew the existing one.

Students, intellectuals, and young workers did become masters—masters of this fragile antisociety. They never became masters of their own society.[6]

Similarly, the Watts riot in the black ghetto of Los Angeles produced this memory in one of its young participants:

In those five days I was right there at the centre between freedom and liberation. It was like an out-of-memory period, where you go into a time capsule, where before you were hoping for freedom within the civil rights movement and when you came out you hoped for liberation. . . .
The people had no control over the Watts riot. It was natural. If someone would say was it organised? I would say no. If they would say was it unorganised? I would still say no. . . . there was no leadership. Watts as a community was the leadership.
A lot of people like to say the Watts riot was a negative thing, but it was a positive thing. I look at it as a symbol of hope.[7]

But that kind of contagious headiness was brief, and the real strength of the social structure they confronted soon made itself known. By 1970 the utopianism had for the most part gone sour, and those organisations that survived to pick up the pieces tended to be characterised by the form that Mannheim identified as 'ideology'. That is, their perceptions were partial, coloured by particular positions or interests. Each of these groups tended to claim ultimacy, yet their competition fragmented the movement to the point where most of the young people who had formed the 'troops' of the movement simply gave up and went home. In Western Europe in particular, while the original movements had faulted both the capitalist and the communist systems of modernity, it was the established parties of the Left that were able to bring order out of chaos and inherit the power of the youth movements. In Eastern Europe, where the Communist power structure was more clearly identified as the enemy, the alternative became identification with the privatistic styles of the counterculture and a backing off from political activism. In America, later student cohorts seemed to acquiesce to the system, and sought to get from it what they could as individuals. The growing conformity among US and Canadian students has elicited a *caveat* from Levitt, however: 'it would be wrong to consider this conformity an expression of passivity or resignation. On the contrary, it is the conformity of contract, wholly formal and instrumental. These students know their rights . . .'[8] For some youth, this kind of distancing is accompanied by a primary identification with the expressive youth culture of the private sphere, and their concern with public issues seems to have been discarded or repressed.

A significant number of youth during the 1970s and early 1980s have become involved in some religious movement or other, some of which are particularly geared to the improvement of their personal lives, others to some apocalyptic approach to social change. The alienation from social institutions that was part of the movement of the 1960s has made it hard for youth to find any positive qualities in the established or 'mainline' religions, but some are attracted to conservative religious groups whose heritage has been that of the sect. Others have turned to Eastern methods of achieving enlightenment, or to religious derivations from psychological self-help groups. Some have been able to recreate the utopian mentality of the early days of the movement in religious groups that strive to bring in a new and godly order.

Others, bitter anarchists, have gone underground, to emerge only when they attempt to strike a blow against the hated establishment. These have fused in recent years with various terrorist groups that sometimes act on their own, sometimes work for governments that oppose those they find the most repressive. But these terrorist activities, for all the negative effect they can provide in the world, seem to be the rear-guard activities of a failed movement.

The movements that seem to be the real inheritors of the youth movements of the 1960s are particular movements of more specialised interest. The women's movement clearly fits into that category, and those of Third World peoples and American Blacks do as well, although the latter, as we have seen, was also a source of the youth movements.

5. THE LARGER QUESTION: YOUTH MOVEMENTS AND CULTURAL CHANGE

We return, then, to the original question of the larger meaning of contemporary youth movements. It is my contention that they were tied to a change of culture that will not go away as have the most apparent youth movements. The university education that has been both the source of concern and the organisational nexus of these movements is a requirement for a culture that is based more and more on high technology and the management of complex organisations. It is the technicians and the managers that are the cultural élite of modern society, and indeed of the culture that some have termed post modern. Class conflict is no longer based so much on the relation to the means of production as on the systems of information and distribution.[9] New definitions of justice and of rights are attaching themselves to distributive equality more than to access to the means of production. The rising élite is not rooted first in the economic structures of society, but rather in the information systems, and at the present time the sources of information tend to be linked to the universities.

It is this that made the universities targets of youthful revolt. However, the changes instituted by the universities in response to that revolt were not the ones that have to be made. Many of them weakened the programmes that lead to mastery of the new culture, giving more persons access to programmes but not to the real sources of power. Much of the unrest on campus resulted from the reduction of emphasis on teaching in favour of research activities. The question may be whether university structures as we know them are truly capable of performing both functions, or whether new institutions either for teaching or research must be created. Traditionally, at least in the faculties of humanities and social sciences, universities have sought to train an élite minority of critical scholars who can offer objective criticisms from the margin of society, free of the claims of any vested interest. Now they are also engaged in training the persons who must make the major social decisions on the basis of some kind of shared societal values. Whether or not they can both maintain the critical objectivity and provide appropriate values for the leaders of a technocratic society remains an issue.

Another issue has to do with the political functions of the nation State. Both the youth culture and the economy of post-modern society have transcended national identification, and the objective reality of modern warfare is that no contemporary nation can defend its own borders. The protest of youth against the nation State can be seen as a natural reaction to an institution that has become outmoded. Finally, both the anti-institutionalism of the youth movements and the turn of some youth to non-traditional religious calls into question the appropriateness of contemporary religious institutions and ideologies. The vision required for moving into a new era almost of necessity fits the definition of religion, not as an institutional form but as a way of responding to the world. For that reason, it is possible to see contemporary youth movements as early indications of a new reformation of the proportions of the Protestant Reformation of the sixteenth century, if not larger, given the realities of today's 'global village'.

Notes

1. Kenneth Kenniston *Young Radicals* (New York 1968) p. 284
2. Milton Viorst *Fire in the Streets: America in the 1960s* (New York 1979) p. 289
3. See Daniel Bell *The Cultural Conditions of Capitalism* (New York 1976)
4. Cyril Levitt *Children of Privilege: Student Revolt in the 1960s* (Toronto, Buffalo and London 1984) p. 46
5. See e.g. Margaret Mead *Culture and Commitment: A Study of the Generation Gap* (New York 1970)
6. Gianni Statera *Death of a Utopia: The Development and Decline of Student Movements in Europe* (New York and London 1978) p. 130

7. Paul Williams, as quoted by Viorst, in the book cited in note 2
8. Levitt, in the book cited in note 4
9. See e.g. Helmut Shelsky *Die Arbeit tun die Arderen: Klassenkampf und Priesterherrschaft der Intellektuellen* (Munich 1977)

Paul Kapteyn

'Even a Good Education Gives Rise to Problems' The Changes in Authority between Parents and Children

1. THE PATHOS OF ALARM

CHILDREN ARE a constant care—and worry—for their parents nowadays and in our kind of society that care has become a matter of conscience. Children ought, we think, to have a good time and, if they do not, those concerned soon feel guilty and become ashamed of each other and of themselves. This sense of public morality is praiseworthy, but it is not without problems. One of them is that the uneasiness increases until it becomes a pathos of alarm, in which 'care of the child' is raised above the level of a conflict of interests and competition and our view of the factual relationship is obscured 'in its interest'.

One example of this alarm can be seen in the theme of this number of *Concilium*: 'Youth without a Future'. The extreme nature of this formula arouses our consciences—if in fact they were asleep—but at the same time sets the tone for the debate before any comment has been made. The editors of *Concilium* are not alone here. This 'good' attitude is present in many other periodicals, newspaper articles and reports by various authorities. The message of parents is: 'Young people are in a bad way' and this is usually followed by a reference to the increasing use of alcohol and drugs and the growing number of suicides and crimes. All this points to 'apathy and aggression', parents continue, and is an understandable reaction to the 'disaster' of unemployment, the 'terrifying' nuclear arms race and so on. The real question, however, is whether the connection between these and other 'catastrophic' aspects of modern society and the plight of young people really exists and whether the seriousness of the problem that is expressed in the extreme choice of language is really in accordance with what in fact happens. With the developments in the Netherlands in mind—a comparison with what is happening elsewhere is outside my scope—the answer to this question is certainly 'no'.

2. DEVELOPMENTS IN THE LONG TERM

In the history of Europe, the 'interest of the child' is an argument that has only very gradually acquired its present compelling force. As other authors in this number have pointed out, age played a subordinate part in social relationships in the past. A person's significance in society was determined by the social strength of the family to which he or she belonged. The result was that some children enjoyed at an early age the power and respect that, according to later norms, belonged exclusively to older people, while some older members of society—the majority—were treated as children and sometimes even called children.

That situation changed. With the rise of national States, violent eruptions within these territories were increasingly controlled by a central authority, with a corresponding increase in internal security. At the same time and together with this change, economic activity expanded and not only security, but also welfare gradually increased. One consequence of this was that there was to some extent a decrease in the differences in power between various groups in the population. This led to those who were most dependent on others—the old, the sick and women and children—becoming less vulnerable.

What was especially important for the relationship between older and younger people was that greater demands were made of the human being's ability to learn within the framework of these changes in society. Economic growth called for a more extensive knowledge of the processes of production and of management of affairs in the widest sense. The increasing importance of the central authority also presupposed a knowledge of the instruments of control. That knowledge had to be formed and handed on and this strengthened the position of young people. They were, after all, the ones who had to be taught that knowledge—in their own interest and in that of the family, the district, the town and the country to which they belonged. And if the handing on of that knowledge was to be successful, older people had to bring young ones up with more attention, care and patience than they had in the past. Young people therefore acquired more power and the balance that had previously been tilted against them gradually moved in their favour.

This development was, moreover, not confined simply to learning in the practical and cognitive sense of the word. The increasing level of knowledge and skill extended to the formation and control of the emotions. Whereas children continued to be what they were—and that was, because of the nature of their biological resources, very impulsive—older people had learned how to control their primary impulses, thus causing the difference between the generations to increase. On the one hand, older people were more strongly moved by what they regarded as the innocence of children and they were convinced that that innocence had to be protected. On the other hand, however, they were frightened by their shameless lack of inhibitions and that had to be carefully watched and restricted. This psychological gap, which was bridged in the course of the educational process, gave greater significance to age as a time of learning in social relationships.

3. RECENT DEVELOPMENTS

It was, to begin with, in the higher levels of society that the special position occupied by children was very marked. Later, other social groups were caught up in the same movement and, in the second half of the nineteenth century, as the result of direct intervention on the part of the authorities, the care of young people from the lower strata of society was also established at a national level. From that time onwards many different laws were enacted concerning education, the penal code, parental power and related matters. In the last decade especially, these laws have been greatly extended, with the result that there have never before in history been so many young people exempted for such a long time from what may be described as civil duties in order to carry out what has become their paramount duty—learning!

We know now that this rapid development has not been the result of carefully considered planning. Such associations of co-operation and competition as NATO and the EEC, which came about as a consequence of the Second World War, have made an extension of compulsory education both possible and necessary as social conditions. At the time, however, there was no plan to expand the learning process nor was there any clear idea of the possible consequences of the increased care of young people or of how what was wanted could be obtained and what was not wanted avoided.

The argument for extending the learning process, expanding social and cultural provisions, establishing a number of youth reception centres and practising greater leniency in the punishment of juveniles and so on—in a word, the argument for extending the care of young people—was conducted mainly in moral terms. It was good to enable more children to learn more and this was a justified aim in itself. Hardly anything was said about the consequences. There were inevitable consequences, of course, but there was at the time no image of social developments in 'retrospect and prospect', with the result that the consequences, when they became apparent, came as an unpleasant surprise.

During the 1970s, public discussion about young people changed in tone. There was less admiration for the vigorous impulsiveness of the young and more care—and worry—that they might be running wild. The 'coming of age' and 'maturity' that had been so praised in the previous decade was now feared as 'anomie' or 'lawlessness'. On the one hand, society became concerned about football hooligans or about obvious forms of petty delinquency. On the other hand, there was increasing anxiety about the equally spectacular appearance in the Netherlands of contentious youngsters who went much further in their protest actions—vandalising private houses and so on—than they had in the early 1960s.

There was also real anxiety about the growing consumption of alcohol and drugs. Compared with the previous decade, this seemed to have assumed much more grim proportions. It seemed also to point to increasing apathy on the part of young people and increasing aggression in criminal acts was often called its psychological counterpart. Finally, the public became more and more aware of youth unemployment especiallly from 1980 onwards. This came to be regarded as the main cause of these phenomena. It completed the sad picture of the youth of today.

However convincing it may seem at first sight, this presentation of the state of affairs is not sufficient to explain the situation. This is simply because the problems mentioned do not run parallel with youth unemployment, which is of a later date. They run side by side with that increasing care of young people to which I have already referred and they have to be seen as the unforeseen consequences of that care.

4. THE BREAKDOWN OF HIERARCHICAL GRADES

This increasing care led to a rapid change in the balance of power between older and younger people. Relationships of authority became less hierarchical and both parties became more dependent on consultation and mutual trust.

This first became apparent in domestic relationships. Parental and especially paternal authority diminished. The father's word of command was no longer compellingly effective or convincing. The nature of the new relationships was most clearly expressed in cases where a conflict between parents and a child continued for so long that the child eventually left home and found accommodation in one of the new youth reception centres financed by the local authority, whose legal obligation was in fact to support parental authority. This kind of case in which the interest of the child was used as an argument received a great deal of attention and threw light on what was happening generally, but was not expressed in most families with the same drastic consequence.

Parents also had to register a similar loss of ground in the case of school life. Not only the extension of compulsory education, but also the growth of all kinds of school activities to include such things as form social evenings, sex instruction, talks about the Third World and nuclear weapons and school camps meant that parents had an even less firm grip on what was being done with and by their children. The school staff became more influential than the parents in the lives of the children, but the control that these representatives of the central authority exercised was, because of the nature of their work, less compelling that of the parents in the past.

The third area in the changing relationships of power and authority was free time. More and more leisure activities took place in officially sponsored sports centres, music schools and neighbourhood and club houses, often only for young people. The same or other youngsters also frequented cafés or discothèques or simply spent their leisure time on the streets. This led to a further collapse of parental authority and, together with the phenomena that I have mentioned above, to the loss of the father's typical privileges. In the Netherlands, those privileges included the right to look first at the newspaper, to go to the toilet first in the morning and to use the familiar form of 'you' to the children, while they had to continue to use the polite form. Parents even lost their claim to be called 'father' or 'mother' and were addressed by the first names.

Parents were, however, not alone in this erosion of authority. The same could be said of teaching staff in the schools. They had, it is true, gained at the expense of parents in opportunities for power, but they could no longer exert their traditional authority over their pupils. In the past, school children knew that the head was the boss. His authority was exercised in a peremptory manner and left very little to chance or to inspiration on the pupil's part. A pupil who did not keep to the school rule to wipe his or her feet before entering the building or to march in ranks of four and led by a teacher when going from one place to another knew that he or she would be told off the first time and punished the second.

This hierarchically structured regime did not lead to a denial or a neglect of 'team spirit'. On the contrary, just as in the family, that mutual solidarity was stressed at school, but it came from the top and the clear intention was to compel the pupils to be obedient by urging them to be united. The 'good name' of the school was at stake! The ideal aimed at was 'harmony', but it was based on 'inequality'. It can therefore be defined as 'harmonious inequality'.[1]

But even this regime changed. Order in schools became less strict and the handing on of knowledge relied less on repetition and memorising and more on insight and comprehension. Older teachers especially had great difficulties in accepting this loss of power and authority and resisted the change. Their protest was, however, of no avail. With the extension of compulsory education and the increasing measures taken to encourage youngsters from lower social groups to learn more easily and for longer periods, a less authoritarian attitude became obligatory even in the daily practice of school life. The old regime aimed at the top level, whereas the new regime was concerned with the lowest. There was less emphasis on competition between the most able and more on solidarity with the weakest members of the group.

Younger teachers had less trouble accommodating themselves to this movement from the top to the bottom, mainly because their self-respect was differently orientated and they were themselves the product of more egalitarian relationships. They were therefore able to regard their association in teaching with socially lower groups as an opportunity to achieve their ideal of a 'harmonious equality'. They saw their teaching, in other words, as work done in their own interest and in the 'interest of the child'. It was a contribution to less hierarchically structured relationships. They hoped that mutual trust would grow between pupils and teachers. Did this in fact happen?

5. POSITIVE RESULTS

A good insight into the consequences of the changes in power between older and younger people is provided by an investigation that took place in 1981 into the changed state of affairs at the lower technical high school in a large Dutch city. This section relies to a great extent on the information given in this report.[2]

The investigation concludes that many forms of direct control have in fact either disappeared or at least weakened within the changed relationships, but that more is demanded in terms of self-control on the part of both pupils and teachers. A further conclusion is that, in general and with a great deal of trial and error, these increased demands have been satisfied and that the level of mutual trust has therefore been raised.

(a) At school

One indication of this is the fact that the extension of compulsory education has been relatively successful. Most schoolchildren come under this legal obligation because of their age and therefore belong to the army of a million members who are dragged out of bed on five mornings each week by a million parents, given something to eat and sent off to school, where they are supervised by tens of thousands of teachers. Looking at the scope of the law governing compulsory schooling, it is possible to think that we have created a Gulag archipelago of educational institutions from which no child can ever escape. This would seem to invalidate the claim that the relationships of power and authority have become less compelling. In fact, control of the survival of compulsory education has become nominal.

It is true, of course, that every local authority has officials appointed to supervise its functioning, but the sanctions that they can impose are no more severe than those applied to driving offences and the control that they are able to exercise is minimal. They can in fact only remind parents and pupils that regular attendance at school is in their own interest. In addition to these officials, the school itself also exercises control over the pupils. Absences are marked in the register and a letter of explanation from the parent or guardian is required in each case of default. In the Netherlands, a pupil is punished if he cannot give a good reason for his absence by detention after school or extra written work at home.

These measures are not very impressive and they are only effective if the pupil goes back to school after his absence. In general, compulsory education is to a great extent based on the expectations of the parents and pupils themselves. This form of self-control seems to be effective—this is clear from the usually good attendance in the Netherlands. There is a general impression that there was less truancy in the past, but, if the great expansion of compulsory schooling is borne in mind, the present figures are quite modest. At a school with more than a thousand pupils, there may be ten or so who are known to escape regularly from the law. About three quarters of the rest of the school population say that they have played truant occasionally, but at the most once a year. In addition, it is worth noting that, of all the pupils to whom the law of compulsory education no longer applies, only an occasional individual in fact leaves school. Most stay on at school until they reach the final class.

We may therefore conclude that success has been achieved in getting more children to learn for a longer period within more egalitarian relationships and that the corresponding demands of self-control have usually been satisfied. As far as the pupils are concerned, this is certainly a great achievement. Most of them in the school investigated in the report mentioned above are the first members of their family to be educated for such a long period. Their parents went to work when they were quite young and therefore behaved quite early in life as adults. Their children are still at school at the same age and are and behave as pubescent adolescents. There is a great deal of difference between the fathers and their sons in their experience of control and compulsion, but this gulf is generally bridged without too many problems. As far as this is concerned, it can be said that socially lower groups have adapted themselves to middle-class behaviour.

Regular school attendance does not, however, mean that all children go to school very willingly. Most of them are conscious of the need to do so and are prepared to conform, although their attitude vacillates between pleasure and displeasure. Problems of order often arise in the second year of secondary education, when Dutch pupils are about fourteen. Younger teachers say that they had most difficulties with classes of this age at the beginning of their career and that they tightened the reins with increasing experience. To begin with, they wanted to associate with the pupils on an equal footing. They tried to get a class that had gone off the rails back into control by admitting that they were wrong, for example, or by appealing for mutual understanding. The general impression, however, is that this moralising exertion of pressure for the ideal of 'harmonious equality' did not work.

All the same, order in class is based more now that it was in the past on mutual trust and respect and more direct means of imposing authority have lost their meaning. An example of this can be found in the rule that apparatus is always checked both before and after a practical lesson to prevent its being lost or stolen. This rule is still adhered to and it is still generally effective. But if something is missing, the teacher is at his or her wits' end. He or she could ask his pupils to turn out the contents of their pockets and bags, but this would be a violation of their self-respect and of mutual trust, so he or she recoils from taking such action. The school therefore has to pay the price of a stolen screwdriver for good relationships.

Another example is provided by the reactions to a situation I suggested to the pupils and teachers in the school where I conducted this investigation. It was based on the following incident. One of the pupils had put a drawing-pin on the teacher's chair. He sat on it, said 'Ow!' and then asked who had played this silly joke on him. No one answered. The teacher then said: 'If one of you is clever enough to put a drawing-pin on my chair, then he ought to be brave enough to admit it. Come on, who did it?' There was still no answer and the teacher finally broke the silence by saying: 'Well, to make up for it, the whole class will have a detention after school today.'

The older teachers who were asked what they thought of this incident said that they too would certainly have punished the whole class in such a case in the past, but that they would not do the same today. They were of the opinion that a collective punishment was no longer in accordance with the modern sense of justice and it was also in conflict with the more egalitarian relationships in schools today. What is more, they said, the pupils simply would not take it. That judgment was echoed by the pupils themselves who were questioned. The problem was familiar to most of them, but they did not agree with the solution of the teacher in the story. They said that they would have admitted it if they had done it and, if they had not done it, they would simply not have stayed behind for the teacher's detention.

The disappearance of this authoritarian method shows that the teacher is now placed in a weaker position. He has to keep a closer eye on his class if he is to know whom he should and whom he should not punish when there is a breach of order. In cases where he is in the dark with regard to who is the guilty party, he can do little more than treat the offence light-heartedly or appeal to the sporting instincts of his pupils not to play such silly jokes again. This, of course, strengthens the position of the pupils. They can feel safe so long as the teacher does not know who the offender is. Most teachers think that there has been no significant increase in cases of disturbing order 'behind the teacher's back'. The conclusion may therefore be on the one hand that teachers must keep a more careful watch on their classes and, on the other, that the respect that they show towards their pupils by not applying collective punishments is rewarded.

(b) Boys among themselves

A similar argument applies to the behaviour of boys among themselves today. When they are together, the most striking aspect of that behaviour is their mutual rivalry and their need to show who is the strongest. It looks very much as though these struggles between boys have more chance to develop now that there is less strict supervision on the part of older people and that the hierarchy of mutual domination that is established in these conflicts has become more important. Older people are often very worried about this. They are afraid of mutual 'terrorisation' and the formation of 'gangs' and there is every chance that this will happen if the groups engaged in fighting are restricted only by the right which the strongest boys claim.

In fact, however there is not much talk of that. Direct prohibition on the part of older people has certainly lost most of its compelling power now, but indirect control in the form of rules which leave the boys free to go their own way has become stronger. It has in fact resulted in the hierarchy of mutual domination remaining in a rudimentary state. I am referring here to the many games and sports organised for the youngsters by older people at the school in which this investigation was conducted and to the role of umpire played by the older people. All these activities are directed towards letting the youngsters experience the emotions of mutual rivalry without any real danger to themselves or others and towards letting them distinguish between what must be taken seriously in life and what must be seen, in contrast to that, as a game. What they should retain afterwards is that their primary emotions have to be restrained in the serious business of life, because the dangers are less imaginary.

Younger boys find it difficult to fulfil these requirements, but these attempts made by adults to teach them through these games show signs of bearing fruit in the case of the older ones. Even in their case, however, the barrier between game and serious living sometimes suddenly breaks down. This conscious or unconscious alternation occasionally occurs when boys are measuring their strength against each other or against adults. This happens especially when one partner is serious and the other is still playing a game or when that game is suddenly taken seriously and that serious living abruptly becomes a game.

These activities with their imitative functions, which are really part of a culture based on games, are practised above all in the sports centres. They also, however, frequently take place in contexts of a less official kind, such as local discothèques or those centres which youngsters use to let the 'poison' be drawn out of them. Sometimes the game aspect of the activity is quite transparent, but there often seems to be more taking place in trend setting establishments. The harsh music and dazzling lighting effects increase the tension for anyone who has not yet acquired disco ears and eyes. The clothes and the whole outward appearance also suggest that very primary emotions of a sexual and aggressive kind are involved here. The young people themselves, moreover, seem to want to go far beyond each other either in passion or in coolness. All the same, there is also a make-believe aspect and the emotions are expressed and evoked but at the same time also controlled. It is true, of course, that some young people lose that ability to keep at a distance from themselves for a shorter or longer period and become drawn into the show, which can no longer be called just a game. But this being drawn in is usually also a game and the majority remain critically reserved towards what is happening to them and around them. The boys are not in any sense fighting a guerilla war, although they sometimes look as though they are. This also applies to all the other 'styles' that circulate from time to time.

This development in rivalry between boys that I have briefly outlined here applies in a certain sense to all young people. Wherever they are, they always learn how to correct their more primary emotions and they have to remember under threat and compulsion what they may and what they may not do and what is permitted as a game or a joke. There are, however, very great differences between how different youngsters behave in different circumstances. Speaking very generally, it is possible to say that, in more hierarchically structured relationships, young people are more inclined to take part in adult life, but usually in a subordinate position and sharing in both the negative and the positive excitements that can be experienced in that life. In less hierarchically structured relationships, on the other hand, children tend more to stay in each others' company, albeit supervised and protected by adults. In relationships of this kind, children have fewer needs and are allowed to do more. They are not subject to the discipline of work and are allowed to 'play'. At the same time, however, they are also allowed to do less and have more obligations. They have to learn and they have also to learn how to respect the limits of the game. They are also not allowed to participate to the same extent in the excitement of adult events. What is more, adult life has itself also lost most of its excitement.

This difference between the past and the present is also revealed in a comparison between Dutch children and those of immigrant families ('guest workers' and people from Surinam). Most of the latter say that they like living in the Netherlands. They seem to be grateful to be here and they are less spoiled and more obedient than Dutch children. But closer examination reveals that there are disadvantages as well. A typical statement is: 'You can go to the discothèque here if you want to, but at home you could go into the fields with your uncle, your father or your brother and kill an animal, prepare the carcass and sell it or eat it yourself. That was really exciting! You can't do that here!' Possibilities of that kind are for the most part banished from our society and are no longer accepted.

The attitude of 'more and less' also gives rise to confusion because light is thrown on only one side of the matter and a judgment is often pronounced on it: 'Young people of today are spoiled and life is much easier for them than it was for us in the past.' The demands that are made of them nowadays are left out of account, yet it is clear from my experience at the lower technical high school that these demands are generally speaking satisfied.

6. NEGATIVE RESULTS

The conclusions drawn in the preceding section may give the impression that the situation has been seen through rose-coloured spectacles, especially in view of the problems that seem to be increasing in the relationships described. One of those problems has already been mentioned. It is, of course, juvenile delinquency.

Delinquency

It is impossible to deny that juvenile crime is on the increase. This was also clearly revealed in my investigation at the technical high school. I had remarkably open talks with the boys and from them it emerged that about ten per cent of them stole mopeds and appropriated other objects that were worth taking. One per cent of them went further along the 'wrong' road and bought and sold stolen goods. Almost all the boys said without much shame that they fairly regularly damaged, vandalised or destroyed other people's property or did shop-lifting. The damage was usually confined to a broken window, or scribblings with a felt-tipped pen and the theft to sweets or 'toys'. But, in view of the fact that so many boys go too far in this way, the total effects are quite considerable and shopkeepers, local government officials and private persons are not complaining of a purely imaginary nuisance.

There is a great deal of concern about juvenile delinquency and one sometimes has the impression that it has become a fundamental social problem. If the recent increase is situated within the framework of the whole change in power and authority between the generations, however, it can be more clearly seen as an annoying phenomenon accompanying a development that can in itself be interpreted positively.

I have already said that, within the framework of more egalitarian relationships, much greater demands are made on self-control and that young people have generally speaking learned how to satisfy those demands. Here, in the context of 'negative results', I would above all emphasise that young people often fail to have sufficient self-control, particularly in cases where these demands apply, but are not made or hardly made as such.

It is perhaps useful to give a brief outline here of the nature of juvenile delinquency today. Young people commit crimes for the most part in public or semi-public places such as supermarkets, telephone boxes, buses and, in the Netherlands, trams and in roads and streets. These places are often called anonymous in the sense that it is not clear who is the boss or who supervises them. But this description is only partly correct. In such places, it is a question not only of weak outside control, but also of the silent expectation that those who use them will be fully in control of themselves.

We do not, after all, live in a country where no one is the boss, where there are no laws or where anyone who wants to can measure his strength against that of others. The very opposite is true. We live in what is above all a civilised country, because there are universal rules which apply to all of us but are not imposed with severe sanctions and close control and which therefore express the trust that those to whom they apply will consent to them and keep them. Most adults fulfil this expectation. In the case of young people, however, there is a discrepancy between the self-control which is silently expected of them and that which they are in fact capable of exerting.

The supermarket provides a very good example of this. If this is compared with the typical shop of only twenty or thirty years ago, the most striking factor is the great reduction in external control. Going shopping today presupposes a greater self-control on the part of the customers. The supermarket has also made it possible for them to do what is called in the Netherlands 'recreational' shopping. The trouble begins, however, when little children are taken shopping. They have not learned to keep their hands to themselves and if their mothers do not watch constantly, they have 'stolen' goods in their hands very quickly. Older children can go shopping on their own and many of them give way to this temptation. The example of the supermarket also shows clearly enough that something, but not very much can be done to counteract the evil of juvenile crime. There can be a tighter control and that has been introduced in recent years. But if shopping is to continue to be enjoyable, there are only limited possibilities for increasing this control.

I said above that juvenile delinquency should be regarded as a phenomenon accompanying a development that ought to be assessed positively. The freedom that adults grant to each other by keeping control of themselves makes them vulnerable to those who have not yet reached that point of development. Their own behaviour is civilised and taken as such for granted, but precisely for that reason they do not see the temptation to which others are exposed and can therefore be said to be 'made blind by civilisation'.

A little more has to be added to this explanation of juvenile delinquency to make it complete. I have outlined the conditions of it, but have not provided a reason for it. In most juvenile crimes, what is in fact stolen is usually of minimal importance. Committing the crime is an end in itself. This desire to be daring would appear to originate in a need for excitement which is met in committing a crime and being afraid of the penalty. As we have already seen, this need can be satisfied by older people directing mutual rivalry between younger ones towards sport and games. Petty crime has to a high degree the function of a game and, what is more, precisely because the difference between what is serious and what is play is not clear in it. The danger that they face in committing a petty crime is experienced as genuine. If they are caught, however, they will say that it was 'just a joke'.

It is, however, not possible to explain all cases of juvenile crime in this way. Petty crime of the kind that I have just described can be regarded as a form of aggression that is 'playful' or 'imitative'. There are, in addition to this, two other forms of aggression which are also based on the discrepancy mentioned above between the self-control that is expected of young people and the self-control that they in fact possess, but which have different reasons.

The first of these I call 'brutal aggression'. This occurs in cases in which the aggressive instincts are subjected to much less strict correction and violence is used to get one's own way. At the technical high school, about one per cent of the pupils behaved in this way. Their sociological background can be described as impoverished. The other form is what I call 'moral aggression'. In this form, violent behaviour is justified by a good aim, such as an attempt to rectify a housing shortage, to create a more healthy environment or to establish peace in the world.

The discrepancy between the self-control that is expected of young people and the self-control that they in fact have is rather more complicated in this case. Because of their education, which is strongly orientated towards equality, these youngsters are sensitive to the ideals of justice and are therefore compelled to make radical decisions. Older people, who have brought them up in this direction, nonetheless expect them to have a relative control over this moral sensitivity. This form of aggression, which does not represent a very serious danger in the Netherlands, although it does in some other countries, is found especially among students. The same feelings were, I detected, present among pupils at the technical high school, but they were less intense and more restricted in their aims.

7. CONCLUSION

This concludes my outline of the recent changes in the position of young people and the possibilities that are provided by and the difficulties that can arise as the result of a good education. I have not dealt with youth unemployment. This is because this is too recent a problem to have had a pronounced effect on the relationship between the generations. It is also because it is clear that young Dutch people at school have, at least until very recently, not yet come to recognise possible unemployment as a problem.

If unemployment continues, however, it will result in a reversion of the present development. The difference in power and authority between the generations will, in other words, increase. In a shrinking employment market, there will inevitably be greater competition for jobs and also for qualifications. However opposed they may be to it, moreover, the older people who dispose of these jobs and qualifications will also have greater opportunities for power. Youngsters will also become increasingly dependent at home, because their opportunities to become independent will inevitably be fewer. There will be an increase in direct control of a more hierarchical kind and this will lead to a decrease in both the possibilities and the difficulties described above. For the time being, however, this change in social attitudes does not seem to have developed so far that what has come about in the past few decades is in danger of being reversed.

Translated by David Smith

Notes

1. I have taken this term from Bram van Stolk and Cas Wouters *Vrouwen in tweestrijd* (Deventer 1983).

2. See Paul Kapteyn 'Een geintje, meester!' *Jeugd en Samenleving* 14 no. 1 (1984) p. 4–37.

PART II

The Economic Dimension

Kees Kwant

Unemployment and Young People in the Netherlands

1. INTRODUCTION

PEOPLE NEED to be needed. I seldom dare say more of a statement than that it applies to all people of all ages, but I suspect that in fact this has a very wide application. We fulfil our need to be needed both in our large-scale and in our small-scale networks of relationships, and in both it takes on very different forms, sometimes rather strange and bizarre ones. In the Western type of modern society people prove themselves in the larger world primarily by means of their job or career. In this way this society is shown to be an organization of work: someone is what he is thanks to his work in the form of a job or career. In the feudal society based on rank and class someone did a certain sort of work because he belonged to a certain class: tasks were linked to class. In our kind of society someone belongs to a certain class because he has a certain kind of job or career. Formerly it was someone's class that determined their work, now it is their work that determines their class.

But it is not yet completely true that people have their job or career to thank for their status. There are artists and writers who have considerable reputations without following a professional career and there are associations which cannot be thought of as professional organisations but the membership of which confers considerable standing. But the standing conferred by a job or career may well count for so much that other forms of status have become marginal. Are not women in danger of being forgotten here? Their standing is indirectly due to career: they acquire standing by marrying someone with a career or profession that confers status. An additional factor here is that to an

37

increasing extent women are no longer satisfied with this indirect status and are themselves concerned to follow a career.

Hence it is not strange that we should find ourselves talking not just of a duty to work but of the right to work: our claim to have a part in things has become a claim to a job or career. In this way education and schooling have more and more taken on the character of preparation for a career. Schooling is primarily directed towards a career and has less to do with the leisure or *schole* from which it got its name. In this situation it is obvious that unemployment, in other words the lack of a structured job or career, is extremely frustrating. Someone who becomes unemployed after his education experiences his education as a bridge ending in mid-air.

This article deals with the influence unemployment has on the way in which young people in the Netherlands make sense of their lives. The subject brings a whole host of difficulties with it. To begin with the beginning and the end of the period of life called youth can vary. It is of course a question of the first years that follow the completion of one's full-time education. The worker with little schooling finishes his formal education in the Netherlands at sixteen, while the medical specialist continues until thirty or thereabouts. So the word 'young' has different meanings when we are talking about a young factory worker and when we are talking about a young specialist. I cannot therefore indicate precisely what is meant here by youth or young people. In the second place, when I distinguish between different groups, I cannot indicate precisely how large these are: their sizes vary according to the movement of the birth-rate and the state of the economy. In the third place I am forced to link the idea of making sense of one's life with large groups when the term seems best suited in relation to individuals. These factors make my subject more difficult to deal with but do not exclude the possibility of having some useful things to say about it.

Although this article focuses on unemployment, I do not confine my consideration simply to the unemployed section of young people. I am convinced that the present situation of long-term unemployment has a profound impact on all young people. I am concerned with the groups that emerge among young people, admittedly always from the point of view of unemployment, and about the way in which the situation of unemployment influences the way in which these different groups make sense of life. From this I hope to draw some conclusions concerning the future of our society.

2. YOUNG PEOPLE IN WORK

The great majority of young people who put themselves on the labour market after finishing their education find work within a short time. Every year at the moment round about 250,000 new candidates are looking for jobs. Of these 180,000 find a job within half a year, but nearly 70,000 young people have to wait for more than a year. Graduates and those who have acquired professional qualifications are not included in these figures. As a rule twenty-three is taken as the upper limit when talking of unemployment among young people. We have already seen that this is an arbitrary limit, since those going on to further education naturally come on to the labour market later. Here too we find increasing unemployment. Already some years ago there was considerable unemployment among biologists, and at the moment unemployment occurs pretty well everywhere, though in differing proportions. There is even a certain number of unemployed doctors. An important reason for unemployment among these graduates is the declining demand for teachers in secondary education: classes are increased in size and the number of teachers goes down. Nevertheless, in pretty well every sector of the world of work, round about 70 per cent of young people seeking a job find one. Of the remaining 30 per cent by no means all are permanently unemployed. But the number of those permanently out of work is not small and is still continuously increasing.

However, it would be completely wrong to think that there is nothing the matter with roughly 70 per cent of young people, that they go on living in the agreeable security of the 1960s, that the freedom from anxiety of that time still remains their lot. They too are affected by unemployment, though in a different way.

In the first place for many of them unemployment is present as a possible and in some cases impending future. Many of them are holding their jobs down while being afraid of losing them.

In the second place—and this is a consequence of the first—these young people stick firmly to their jobs or careers to a much greater extent than was formerly the case. A value that goes unchallenged easily becomes a matter of course to which no one pays any attention any longer. On the other hand people cling firmly to values that are under threat. This has important consequences for behaviour. People do all that is possible in order to let it be seen that they are fit for their job. People thus feel themselves compelled from within to greater dedication to the work demanded of them by their job or career. This explains why there has been a spectacular drop in time off work caused by illness. People are now working with a devotion that can turn into hanging on to their jobs like grim death.

Added to this in the third place is the increasingly close definition of jobs and careers. It has become more difficult for employers to have jobs to offer. For that money has of course to be offered, but once money is at stake people naturally want to know as clearly as possible what they are getting for it.

Hence the requirements of a job or career are more sharply defined and its fulfilment examined more closely. The dedication to the job that we have just been talking about is thus not just something growing from within but is also imposed from outside.

In the fourth place, all this leads to a noteworthy attitude that can be described as pride in one's job. Having a job is no longer something to be taken for granted and is thus experienced as a privilege. One has to exert oneself more than formerly in order to enjoy this privilege. Precisely because one does more for it the idea can creep in that one deserves to belong to those with jobs or careers. My opinion is that this feeling is in the air and is on the increase. While this feeling is positive in character it has a negative side to it. It contains as a kind of implication the idea that those without a job 'deserve' their lot. Of course, when those with jobs have made themselves fit for them through their own efforts those without jobs seem to be not fit for any job. If heaven is earned by those who live there, then those who remain outside have also earned that fate. The pride in their job of those with jobs involves a certain trampling on the unemployed. There is of course an element of truth in all this. There is a number of young people who enjoy such all-round ability that they will certainly find a job and a career, while on the other hand there is a number of people who have so little ability that it is unlikely that they will ever find a job. One can say that the first lot deserve a job and that the others call their fate down on themselves. But we cannot lay down as a general truth that all deserve their fate. Many people become unemployed through the disappearance of the social entity that provides their chance of work: that affects equally those better and those less equipped for their jobs. It also happens that people get jobs thanks to opportunities and influences that are not available to others. The myth that the unemployed are misfits or rejects is thus socially unfair.

Young people who are working are thus profoundly influenced by the situation of unemployment. The importance of what has been said so far will become apparent when we deal directly with the unemployed.

3. THREE GROUPS AMONG YOUNG PEOPLE IN WORK

In view of my terms of reference I need to pay special attention to the question of meaningfulness. Keeping this in view I think we can distinguish three groups among young people in work. These groups are on the one hand clearly present, but they cannot be sharply distinguished from each other and it is difficult to give any numerical estimates of their relative strength.

(a) First of all there are those who are strongly motivated by the jobs or careers they have. What is involved here is those young workers who are not just anxious to hold down a job, like pretty well all workers, but who above this like the work they have to do because of their job or career. This does not have to mean that they are happy in their work all the time from first thing Monday morning till last thing Friday evening. We can pretty well exclude the idea that what we have to do and what makes sense always coincide. No child is in itself always happy to attend every lesson, nor is someone always happy in their work. But many people enjoy doing their work more than is general and feel it is a way of realising themselves: they appreciate that their work compels them to develop their capacities. Briefly, their work makes them more human, even if not all their potentialities are realised within their work. How many workers of this kind are there? Here there is a sharp divergence of opinion between pessimists and optimists. In the Netherlands Hans Achterhuis, for example, takes a gloomy view and regards such workers as being as rare as white crows. The vast majority of workers are like beasts of burden slaving away because of the continually recurring need of subsistence. But surveys point in the opposite direction. Asked if they find fulfilment in their work, very many say they do. Indeed, the majority of workers have a positive evaluation of their work. But the objection can be made that we cannot build too much on this kind of answer. If you ask people if their marriage is satisfactory, their children presentable, their life agreeable, then will not very many say 'yes' even when their experience is profoundly the reverse? Nor is an affirmative answer necessarily a lie, since many hide their misfortunes from themselves. In brief, there is no guarantee that people are what they say they are. As far as I am concerned it is completely impossible to work out empirically how large the group is that I am considering here. I would simply presume that it is fairly large. These people are attached both to their job or career and to their work. (b) Then there is a second group of conscientious workers. By these I mean workers who are attached to their jobs, as everyone is from time to time, but who do not find any great fulfilment in their work and who for external reasons are nevertheless tied to their work for personal reasons in a positive way. They find that they have to work, that they are obliged to do so. This occurs in two ways. First of all a social tradition can play a role here. Many have the idea from their social environment that they must work. We can almost talk of a Kantian categorical imperative. Rational considerations do not play the leading role here. 'It's definitely settled' that one must work without any thought of someone actually having established this point. I myself was born and grew up in an environment of this kind. It was definitely established that we had to work. The question of the inner meaning of work was simply not asked. The necessity and the meaning belonged to different orders. We grew up in such a way that we learned not to pay any attention to our likes.

In the second place religion can play a role in this. It is pretty definite that Calvinism, for example, contributes to a great degree to the work ethic, i.e. to the idea that working is a duty. When religion and social tradition support each other, the necessity becomes firmly and unshakably established.

In the Netherlands, originally an agrarian country influenced by Calvinism, this group was pretty large. In this case the meaning of work is definitely established, even apart from any experience of meaning. The absence of the latter does not affect the meaning of work. There is as it were a belief in meaning independent of any experience of it. People then practise a kind of asceticism in order to accept their work as a positively meaningful thing against the evidence of their experience. This may sound crazy, but we are dealing here with a piece of social reality.

(c) Finally there are those willing to work without enjoying it, workers who are keen on their jobs or careers and ready to do the work involved without being motivated to do it either by experiencing it as meaningful or by believing it to be so in the way we have just discussed. Their experience of their work is negative, and they do not hide this experience from themselves nor, to some extent, from others. They want to keep their jobs and so are ready to work, but in such a way that they regularly curse their work and are beginning to look forward to Friday evening on Monday morning. They are in the tragic situation of a considerable portion of their life being taken up by work that does not bring them any genuine fulfilment. They are compelled to seek the meaning of their life outside their work, in which 'entertainment' above all plays a part. They live on bread and circuses that they hope to find outside their work, often for little money. Some observers contend that the number of people of this kind is alarmingly high, among them Achterhuis. Although I do not share their pessimism, nevertheless I am afraid that their number is not inconsiderable.

(d) There is a number of developments which arise with regard to these various groups. The most notable in my view is that the second group is growing smaller, most probably because the links with tradition and the influence of religion are diminishing. The old blind belief in work was present above all in the agrarian milieu, and thus in the villages. But at the moment the villages are becoming less village-like. As far as religion is concerned, it is an established fact that Church affiliation is on the decrease. It was above all the traditional religions organised in the Churches that underlined the work ethic. The new forms of religiosity that are rapidly emerging—and sometimes also disappearing—are not so strongly behind the work ethic. Where do those who are no longer bound by religion and tradition find their way to? My fear is that they move into the third rather than the first group, and so I am afraid that this third group is on the increase. This is also the case for another reason: the forms of work between higher creative work on the one hand and simple routine performance on the other are on the decline thanks to the third industrial revolution connected with the microchip and the computer. Hence our world of work is becoming characterised by an impending dichotomy of groups 1 and 2.

4. THE JOBLESS

The following groups can be distinguished among the jobless:

(*a*) Those who are expelled but are still in touch. The unemployed are expelled from the world of work. The Dutch government demands of them that they go on trying to remain connected to it. They must go on demonstrating that they belong to the world of work, that they are destined to have a job or career. It is expected of them that they should give expression to this attitude, and this by going on looking for a job even when their chances are slender. Many comply with this desire, not so much because they are obedient to an external authority as for internal reasons: they themselves want nothing better. They go on looking for a job and regard the period of unemployment as an unwanted interim period which will come to an end. They are outside the world of work without having left it mentally. It is pretty well self-evident that they find it difficult when the world of work does not offer them any real prospect any more. The government goes on holding out the prospect of a future of full employment, even if it is in a distant future.

(*b*) There are those unemployed who, probably without abandoning the idea of a job completely as a possible future, nevertheless seek a provisional solution in order to prove themselves socially, and do this by devoting themselves to alternative work, i.e. to work which claims to be socially useful without having the distinction of being recognised as a job or career. This happens in a number of different ways.

First, there is alternative work that is arranged by, or at least in consultation with, the authorities. It is obvious that the authorities have an interest in this kind of thing since on the one hand there is much work waiting to be done and on the other there are people drawing benefits while going round without work. Here we are of course threatened by the spectre of 'work creation'.

Secondly, there is alternative work that arises from individual initiative, outside the legal framework without thereby coming into conflict with the law. The term used is the grey economy. There are entrepreneurs who are able to link work and workers in cases where our world of work breaks down.

Thirdly, there is the work provided by the black economy. Work that is done within the world of work but has become uneconomic for many is then done outside it against payment but at rates well below those obtaining within the official economy. It is well established that an awful lot of work is done in this way in the Netherlands.

Finally, there is the alternative work that is done in the so-called underworld. Just as our towns have sections above and below ground, so our social world has a section above ground and an underworld. The underworld cannot flourish in small villages but is rather an urban phenomenon. In this underworld a kind of underground world of work is encountered where functions are bestowed and quasi-jobs can be distinguished. Think for example of the organisations that exist around the traffic in drugs, of the growing number of organised gangs. There are some unemployed who live above ground but work underground. I know for sure that this phenomenon is spreading, but I am not very well in touch with it. I ask myself how this dimension of social reality can be studied empirically. All kinds of events indicate that something like the underworld does not exist merely in the dimension of ordinary theft but also in the major sphere of international financial dealing and management. The Mafia demonstrates the extent and patterns the underworld can have and how great its importance can become.

(c) Finally, there are the unemployed who have broken free from the world of work. This seems to happen in various ways.

There are the unemployed who do this consciously and deliberately. This is for example the case with those who join together to form the alliance against the work ethic. Their view is that the unemployed can only create a new future for themselves when they have freed themselves from the strong mental links to the world of organised jobs and careers.

Beyond this there are many who do not put things in such a principled way but who simply give themselves over to the forms of relaxation that are accessible. In this music, alcohol and drugs play a large part. It is fairly obvious that in this context it is easy for an aggressive attitude to emerge with regard to a society which has become an organised world of work and in which one has become a stranger. It is clear, too, that in this case it is easy for links to be formed with the underworld.

(d) It seems to me that this last group, formed by the unemployed who detach themselves from the world of work, is growing steadily. It is obvious that it is above all the long-term unemployed who belong to it; and the long-term unemployed that there are remain unemployed while every year a fresh draft is added to their number. That this is so is apparent among other things from the change in attitude on the part of the labour exchanges: they have given up trying to act on behalf of all the unemployed in looking for work because the group of 'hopeless cases' was gradually becoming too large.

The first group, which I have labelled the expelled who are still in touch, grows during unfavourable circumstances but diminishes somewhat when there is some improvement in conditions. The chief characteristic of this group is that its membership is constantly changing. New people join it, but many drop out because they have found work.

The number of people, finally, who devote themselves in one way or another to alternative work is growing steadily. In Amsterdam alone they can be numbered in five figures, and over the country as a whole there are certainly more than 100,000 people who in one way or another are engaged in the grey or black economy. I am inclined to suggest that, when we add it all up, their number would exceed 150,000.

5. PROGNOSES BASED ON THE PRECEDING ANALYSIS

In the foregoing two comparatively large groups of frustrated young people clearly emerge, first those who are willing to work but do not enjoy it, and then the unemployed who have detached themselves from the world of work. They remain affected, of course, by our Western work ethic that is in the air they breathe and has also been internalised by them. They too have been brought up and educated to think in terms of a career and a job. The situation of these two groups is very different. Those who belong to the first have a job and share in all the rights linked with that. The others have the dole and are noted down as people looking for work. But they also have a lot in common. First and foremost there is the lack of enjoyment with regard to the world of work. Then there is the need to look for the meaning of their life outside work, in which context we should think primarily of entertainment and of social contacts with those in the same state as themselves. A third factor they have in common is that they are not well off: the difference between the minimum wage and the dole is not so amazingly large. These young people are thus drifting away from many current patterns of making sense of one's life. Jobs and careers and respect for these do not count for very much with them. Leisure time is no longer a change with regard to work that nevertheless remains closely connected with it. Most cultural values hardly have any meaning for them, and the only passages that interest them in the Queen's speech are those that affect their income. The government and politics have for them an overwhelmingly negative significance. How large are these two groups put together? In my view we should be thinking in terms of pretty well a million people in receipt of an income. If we count in members of their families, then we are dealing with millions of people who are drifting away from the spirit of our society and are becoming alienated from it. They cannot be regarded as candidates for emancipation because they do not really want to become involved with that. Their presence is also clearly noticeable in the educational system: our schools, too, are inhabited by apathetic young people who can be regarded as junior members of the two groups mentioned here. Naturally there is no question here of clearly defined boundaries. What are involved are groups with a distinct core but fading towards the edges.

This serious phenomenon may indicate that the world of work is becoming the preserve of an élite. It has become a privilege to be able to share in it. What we are saying is that there is a large group that is barred from this privilege, and this group threatens to take on permanent form. The world of work includes a sub-section of poor bloody infantry who legally still belong to it but mentally hardly do so any longer. People collect the pay all right but do not like the work or the obligation to work. They hang on reluctantly, among other things because they do not want to lose their job because of the income it represents. A section of the population is emerging which is either included in the world of work or dangling against its underside. During the 1950s we were coming to think that our society was itself a world of work, that our population and the staffing of the world of work would overlap. Now an end seems to be coming to this because the world of work is becoming a matter of an élite, at least when we look at its general staff, its officers giving orders and that portion of its personnel that is heart and soul committed to it. In this sense we can perhaps say that the world of work is growing apart from the general population. It has not yet reached this point, but this is the direction we are going in. Already there is a large section of young people that is living apart from the world of work.

It is a normal phenomenon that the élites of society make use of their position in order to enrich themselves, often in an unreasonable way. This can happen even when in an earlier phase they have protested against previous forms of enrichment and the inequality that flows from these. Something of this kind is now happening once again. The entrepreneurial middle classes who form the basis of our world of work protested against feudal inequality and the forms of enrichment that went with it. But our world of work, even in this phase, is not free from the ancient evil. Its élite, the new élite of the new society, is once again enriching itself in a fairly spectacular manner: the top salaries of our world of work are rising to great heights, and even to heights that are not made public. There is no guarantee that the new inequalities that are emerging will be less hard and less unacceptable than those that were relegated by the bourgeois-liberal revolution. These inequalities are incidentally also emerging in Communist societies. It is striking that the present Dutch government says it is in principle an advocate of the new inequalities and of the differentials that are defined as a reversal of levelling down: such a policy includes the idea that equality should once again be defined as a danger and inequality as a desideratum for the future. If you look on the one hand at the level of minimum wages and minimum benefits and on the other at top salaries (to the extent that these are visible), then it becomes clear what forms the new inequality is taking and on what level the new élite is placing itself. If the world of work becomes in this way a matter of an élite, then it is growing apart from society as a whole, is breeding a new substratum under itself and thus is creating a new danger of subversion. The new substratum already exists but does not yet have a name. It is not yet distinct enough as a unity to bear a name already. A not inconsiderable part of young people is being pushed into this new substratum. It is unnecessary to add that substratum and underworld do not coincide, even if parts of both can overlap.

Al Hatton

An Analysis of Youth Unemployment and Future Prospects for Jobs. The Case of Canada

DESPITE THE fact that the issue of youth unemployment has probably become the number one social problem in Canadian society at this time, no national consensus has been reached in finding a way to moderate its intolerable effects.

In order to appreciate the profound nature of the youth unemployment dilemma in Canada, it is important to present a brief overview of the economic conditions which have combined to dramatise both the issue and its effects on the consciousness of Canadians.

1. THE ECONOMY

In Canada, as in other Western capitalistic societies, the mass industrialised economic structure envisioned to benefit all citizens is in decline. A brief description of the factors which have caused this slowdown will shed light on this complex situation and suggest some innovative responses required for practitioners to balance off the repercussions of the economic breakdown.

First, the Canadian economy has been dependent on cheap non-renewable resources such as oil, which in the early seventies began to escalate in cost. The second factor which Western economies have witnessed over the past twenty years is a concentration of wealth and a proliferation of Transnational corporations and banks. These large enterprises moved capital to countries where labour is cheaper, corporate taxes lower and environmental standards minimal. Third, there has been a shift of emphasis from the manufacturing sector to the information industries, throwing thousands of skilled labourers out of work while technological advances have displayed workers and shut down numerous plants. There has also been increasing competition from Third World countries leading to mass lay-offs in selected industries such as textiles.

This situation has been exacerbated by the responses of both government (at all levels) and the private sector. Governments have borrowed heavily from future generations to cushion Canadians from the worst effects of these developments. They have also encouraged protectionism in selected industries, blunting individual enterpreneurial capacity. The pervasive philosophy in response to these changes has been for government to develop policies which fight inflation or patiently wait for the American economy to improve thereby increasing investment in Canada.

Unfortunately, human labour is not a vital variable in this type of equation. The private sector has responded primarily by mergers; downsizing to improve competitiveness and profitability or moving to more lucrative locations. There is a fond hope in many circles of Canadian society that business is the motor of the economy (too much government involvement has been a major cause of our economic woes) and every effort is being encouraged to support business growth.

This may increase business profitability at best and moderate the problem to some extent. However, it will not address the fundamental issue of job creation, nor direct these new jobs towards the poor, the handicapped and the otherwise marginalised in our society.

Nature and scope of youth unemployment

In the midst of all these changes confronting our society and shifting our perceptions and values, the massive problem of youth unemployment crept up on most policy analysts and decision-makers in our country. The numbers affected by this problem are magnified by the youth at the tail end of the baby boom who are just now being integrated into the system and have grown up associating progress with normalcy. In addition, from 1966 until today, female participation in the workplace has gone from 38 per cent to 50 per cent. This year, there will be as many women as men enrolled in post-secondary educational institutions. Finally, in 1967, 87 per cent of all immigrants were from the US and from European countries and, by 1977, the percentage had shrunk to 47 per cent with 53 per cent arriving from Third World countries. Canadians have not developed policies to adequately respond to these recent demographic shifts.

In March 1984, there were 1,541,000 unemployed in Canada, of which 557,000 or 36.1 per cent were in the age group 15 to 24 years. The rate of unemployment for this age was 20.3 per cent, substantially higher than the national average rate for all ages of 12.7 per cent. In Newfoundland, the unemployment rate for 15 to 24 year olds was 39.9 per cent. In addition to the youth who are included in these *official* figures of 'unemployed', there is a significant number of hidden or discouraged unemployed who are not looking for work. Realistic figures suggest the number is closer 700,000 young people out of work in Canada.

A general analysis demonstrates that unemployment rates are higher for males than females, and increase for adolescents over 20–24 year olds. The severely unemployed tend to be those with the least education (school drop-outs) who live in slow growth regions. Unemployment among native youth is particularly acute, with unemployment rates more than three times those for non-native youth.

2. THE EFFECTS

The social costs of a persistent, high level of structural unemployment include both the direct and measurable costs of unemployment insurance and welfare as well as the loss of the product generated if unemployed youth were usefully employed. A myriad studies and recent articles highlight increasing suicide among the young, high levels of delinquency, drug and alcohol abuse as well as stress. The majority of these characteristics are attributed to the issue of youth losing confidence in a healthy future for themselves in terms of work.

A far more insidious and intangible process is also occurring which is alarming professionals involved with this population. It is the cynicism, apathy, hopelessness and alienation which chronic unemployment breeds. Deprived of social contacts attained from meaningful work, young people lose touch with the values of the workplace, eventually drifting towards the margins of society.

In response to this intolerable crisis, one would normally expect some type of political response on the part of youth. However this has not materialised in any sigificant way.

Instead recent surveys and questionnaires suggest that the perceived source of unemployed youth's plight resides within themselves as, for example, in their lack of training and experience. They are inclined to cite personal deficiencies, not broader structural factors in the economy and society, as the cause of their predicament. The result is a passive and individualistic withdrawal from society. It then becomes problematic to envision strategies to implicate these youth in resolving their own problems.

3. GOVERNMENT RESPONSE

Governments in Canada have mounted a large and complex array of programmes aimed at job creation, training, counselling and other means of assisting the unemployed. In the fiscal year 1983–4, the federal government spent about $1.2 billion for improving employment prospects for young people. In the province of Ontario, the government funded youth employment programmes for an additional $123.1 million in the fiscal year 1983–4. The combined costs of federal, provincial and municipal governments towards unemployment insurance and welfare benefits amounted to a staggering $3 billion annually directed toward the young unemployed.

Federal programmes can be sub-divided into two principal divisions: the National Training programme and the job creation programmes. The National Training programme gives priority to training for occupations in demand in the labour market and is targeted at upgrading basic education, occupational skills, job readiness, apprenticeship and language training. There is also money available to provide assistance to employers for employees' training. Another programme, the 'Skills Growth Fund', provides capital dollars to improve facilities or purchase equipment which will accelerate skill development.

There are four job creation programmes targeted at specific sectors most adversely affected by the economic downturn of recent years. 'Canada Works' is a short term seasonal measure to deal with the immediate effects of the recession. 'Local Employment Assistance and Development (LEAD)' is aimed at increasing the number of permanent jobs in communities with high chronic unemployment. 'Job Corps' is intended to provide severely employment disadvantaged individuals with the life-skills and employment related skills to make them 'job ready'. 'Career Access' is designed to enable individuals to obtain work experience by subsidising wages to employers.

The government also has employment offices and a wide array of information systems and packages stretching across the country. The provincial governments also spend millions on employment related services. Obviously the governments of Canada are involved deeply in the issue of youth unemployment and have directed massive funds to alleviate the ill-effects of the crisis.

4. IMPACT OF GOVERNMENT RESPONSE

Generally it must be said that some of the programmes and strategies developed by the government have accomplished their intended goals.

However, there are a number of concerns emerging as the problem of youth unemployment has not abated in the light of larger amounts of money being devoted to cushioning its negative effects.

Some of these are outlined in an 'Ontario Manpower Commission' study which identified that:

less than 10 per cent of federal and provincial programmes directed towards youth are intended for persons outside the education system; the majority of programmes do not provide intensive counselling, assessment and job-matching deemed a particularly critical need for those unemployed youth who are economically and/or socially disadvantaged. programmes (particularly those operated by the Federal government) have been developed on an *ad hoc* basis; there is no central administrative responsibility for provincial youth employment initiatives, thereby making the harmonising of federal and provincial efforts very difficult; evaluation of existing youth employment programmes are limited.

The report also criticised the education system for courses in secondary schools that may not prepare some youth for the labour force and for the system's inability to significantly improve the retention rate in school. There is also a tremendous lack of knowledge about existing programmes for small businesses and young people. The attitude prevalent among many employers is that there is too much 'red tape' involved in working with governments while young unemployed people generally feel suspicious of government offices. Another body of criticism revolves around the short-term 'band-aid' type of approach inherent in many of these programmes. Though they provide short-term relief they are not aimed at attacking the root cause effects of the problem.

Coupled with this argument is the escalating costs of the safety net of benefits created to protect those least able to cope. These include medicare, unemployed insurance, welfare, employer subsidies, expanding training programmes, etc. These programmes may be creating overly protected individuals and a dependence attitude which results in a loss of responsibility, ambition, confidence and optimism—essential ingredients in ensuring that those most directly affected are involved in helping themselves overcome this problem.

5. WHAT CAN BE DONE

The most obvious and agreed upon solutions are for the current economic environment to change; for small businesses and large corporations to reinvest their profits; for governments to lower interest rates and give businesses new tax breaks causing the economy to expand, for job creation to take place; for wages to increase and consumerism to flourish. Some economists claim this to be the only solution while others disagree. However, a consensus has not emerged, and even if this type of shift in thinking and behaviour does occur, there is very strong evidence to suggest that those most in distress would not be the beneficiaries of such a turnaround.

Another likely scenario is that government, at the same time as they try to encourange traditional business development, will also increase the number and variety of safety net benefits and special programmes for those most adversely hit by the effects of a slow growth economy. As pointed out earlier, this has been how the government has responded to date as the crisis has deepened.

Even as we are devoting current energy and money to these approaches, there is an increasing body of analysts and decision-makers who are sceptical about its success.

I believe the solution to the dilemma of economic revival and youth unemployment lies in a wide array of strategies and approaches. The first general category includes:

work-sharing;
tax incentives to encourage employers to create new jobs—a portion targeted at young workers;
pensions to reduce the supply of older workers;
paid-leaves to promote learning and create job openings;
a shorter work week;
support employment subsidies not investment aids;
support small business development over subsidies to large corporations where minimal job creation is occurring at present.

In addition to these ideas, there are a number of examples of how various institutions and groups are responding to the issue of youth unemployment.

The Canadian Chamber of Commerce is in the process of setting up committees across Canada comprised of representatives from business, local government, education, community organisations and labour to work together to combat youth unemployment through improved training and/or job creation.

Another interesting model is an organisation called Katimavik where youth are enrolled in a nine month programme to work on community projects for $1 a day (free room and board). At the end, they receive $1,000 to help them re-enter the work force.

Another movement which is growing slowly are support groups of the unemployed where members combine political lobbying with the provision of necessary services for other unemployed i.e. counselling, organising food banks, helping secure social assistance benefits, sponsoring public meetings, etc.

Across the country, there are a variety of training and work experience programmes which target those youth most disadvantaged. These include computer assisted instruction programmes, pioneered by the Control Data Corporation focusing on skill upgrading, job readiness and search skills.

The Canadian YMCA has also been actively involved in working with unemployed young people since 1969 in Toronto through their YES programme (Youth Employment Services) in training and placement activities. In late 1983, the National Council of YMCAs has broadened their interest in the issue by establishing the 'YMCA Job Generation' programme which will work with disadvantaged youth in 10 cities from coast to coast focussing on life skills enhancement, work experience, job placement and job creation.

The second category of models exist at present at the fringes of acceptable economic activity. These experiments or experiences are not known about, or if known, are not assessed and fed into the mainstream of acceptable 'business' and are not recognised as transferable across communities or other economic sectors. All of these alternatives share a common underlying perspective which is fundamental to understand. It is that those most directly affected must evaluate their situation and decide what they are going to do to improve their condition. The solution does not really lie outside themselves nor is someone going to intervene and solve their problem—not government, nor a large corporation, nor a funder, nor a consultant. Therefore whether it is an individual looking for work, a small group trying to set up an enterprise or a community trying to survive, there must be the will to break down those barriers which inhibit them from developing their own unique solutions. Rarely have these methods been experimented with as a creative response to the particular crisis of youth unemployment.

The first option is that of *cooperatives*. The Cooperative Union of Canada describes a cooperative as 'a business organisation owned by those who use its services, control of which rests equally with all members, surplus earnings of which are shared by members in proportion to the use they make of the service'. Cooperative operating principles stress open and voluntary membership, democratic control (one member, one vote), limited interest or capital, refunds to members, and cooperative education for members. Across Canada today, more than nine million Canadians are members of over 10,000 cooperatives and credit unions whose combined assets exceed $45 billion. What is of particular interest in our country is that the cooperative movement, has flourished when economic conditions are most dire and has happened in isolated, resource poor areas among groups without the so called 'capacity' to succeed.

The cooperative philosophy with its blend of social and economic perspectives should be ideally suited and promoted as one vehicle for connecting the unemployed and acting as a catalyst for energising them to create new enterprises.

In a variety of settings, the *Community Development Corporation (CDC)* has been an effective stimulus for local economic development. The CDC is a self help organisation that attempts to develop structures which combine the social with the economic 'under the umbrella of a locally controlled non-profit corporation'. A strong business division uses the best techniques of the private sector to create viable, productive businesses. Profits from these businesses are reinvested in the activities of the social development and cultural divisions. CDCs often allocate a portion of their profits to a venture capital fund formed with private and public monies to develop high risk enterprises in the community. There are currently approximately 200 CDCs in Canada and they have succeeded in demonstrating that they are effective vehicles for developing viable businesses, local employment and human resources, as well as for the brokering and delivery of appropriate social and cultural programmes. One of the best established CDCs in Canada is New Dawn Enterprises Ltd of Sydney, Nova Scotia. New Dawn has been directly or indirectly responsible for the creation of approximately 1000 jobs and has accumulated assets projected at $12 million for 1984. It has been responsible for constructing a 927 bed senior citizens' residence, renovating two group homes, establishing three dental clinics and local autoparts and pottery businesses.

A third type of strategy to spur economic activity, promote job creation and diminish youth unemployment is *the business incubator model*. The centres are usually located in a large building, sometimes a converted warehouse or school especially in areas where warehousing or education demands are decreasing. Fledgling industries and struggling entrepreneurs are encouraged to locate in the centre through the provision of short term, low cost leases. Frequently, centralised services such as security, utilities, telephones and secretarial are offered. The incubator model provides the perfect setting for bringing together business people with good ideas and local unemployed workers in search of work while providing them with the opportunity to develop new skills. Funds to acquire the centre may be private or public with the municipality often renting any unused building for $1 per year. Surprisingly this idea has not taken off in Canada, although there are similar models operating in the US and Europe. The business incubator model can be creatively adapted and localised to furnish a novel response to the particular needs of the unemployed.

Another interesting experiment is being conducted in Canada, in Halifax, Nova Scotia. There, HRDA Enterprises Ltd is exploring productive alternatives for public transfer payments. Some $200,000 in social assistance money was diverted from the welfare budget of the Social Planning Department of the city to a non-profit corporation (HRDA) which used the money to start businesses that created jobs for transfer payment recipients. As of March 1981, HRDA Enterprises Ltd includes a window cleaning service, a property management company, a commercial book-keeping service, a commercial printing business and a used car franchise. HRDA using welfare dollars as salary, negotiates the hiring of recipients with private sector employees. HRDA has created 55 jobs, 36 were filled with people once deemed unemployable—former mental patients and disadvantaged single parents.

In all of the above instances, there is an underlying belief in the capacity of the unemployed to take charge of their destiny and create new options which have up to now been denied them. This is the fundamental starting point which must be grasped by those working on behalf of young people and by youth themselves. Without such visions and a belief in people's innate capacities, the drift towards dependence, resignation and acceptance will continue and new models and creativity will be stifled.

Bibliograhy

WDR Eldo *Mobilisation for Work: Generating Employment opportunities for Canada's youth* Canadian Chamber of Commerce, Ottawa, Canada.

Jackson, E.T. *Community Economic Self-Help and Small Scale Fisheries*, June 1984 Department of Fisheries and Oceans, Government of Canada, Ottawa.

Canadian Conference of Catholic Bishops *Ethical Choices and political challenges* 90 Parent Avenue, Ottawa, Ontario, K1N 7B1.

Canadian Council on Social Development: *Perception* August 1984 Ross Laver *Young and Out of Work*, McLean's Magazine 16 July pp. 34–39.

Hawken, Paul *The Next Economy* (1983) Holt, Rinehart and Winston, New York.

Juan Andrés Peretiatkowicz

The Effect of Being out of Work on Young People in Chile

'BESIDES PROVIDING financial support, work gives human beings something more basic: it makes them grow. They are born naked, bearing the seeds of a thousand possibilities and the effective reality of none. For these seeds to grow into a tree and bear fruit, the individual must measure him- or herself against nature, against other individuals, transforming them and being transformed by them in his or her turn . . . Each person is what others tell him he or she is or what their attitude shows him or her to be. He or she can also be what others refuse to recognise him or her as . . . (People out of work) do not measure up to nature or to other people, they simply float in a linear space with no centre of gravity. The place where they hide the sorrow and shame of not being, is their house . . . with the doors shut.'[1]

1. SOME FIGURES[2]

To understand the seriousness of the problem in its full extent, we need to know some statistics. Lack of work is one of the problems which a decade of neo-economic liberal economics has failed to solve—which have, in fact grown to previously unheard-of proportions since the installation of the military regime. The percentage of unemployment has generally remained above 10 per cent, reaching 15 per cent in 1975–6 and growing to more than 20 per cent in the present crisis. Of these numbers, it is calculated that during the period 1975–82, young people under the age of 25 made up between 40 and 45 per cent.

Before 1973, the unemployment percentage for the 14–19 age group was between 12 and 18 per cent, rising to a good 25 per cent after the military coup, and to over 45 per cent in the two periods of crisis (1975–6 and 1982); this means that almost half the young people in this age group eligible to join the labour force were without work.

For the 20–24 age group, unemployment was around 10 per cent before 1973, after which it rose to over 25 per cent in the 1975–6 crisis and has stayed almost permanently over 20 per cent (except in 1981). During 1982, it went up to over 35 per cent.

2. CONSEQUENCES

What are the consequences of this situation for the young people who experience it, either through being out of work themselves, or as members of families in which the father is out of work?

On the family level, one of the first effects to be noted is the prolongation of 'youth' through being out of work, the prolongation of dependence. 'The effect is that, despite having gone through the processes proper to the period of adolescence, the young person does not achieve the autonomy which a defined social role would entitle him or her to.'[3] Once they have finished their educational process (or before), young people are faced with the need to contribute economically to their families, by becoming permanent members of the work force; it is this step that determines their incorporation into adult life, that makes it possible for them to realise their life project, which has till then only existed in the sketchiest form. Being out of work strangles this plan at birth, keeps them in a state of dependence, prevents them from taking their place in a world which evaluates people by what they do.

'Some of the effects on personality can be seen in loss of self-confidence and self-appreciation, in a generalised sense of frustration, which in the long run, when they have been out of work for a long time, or repeatedly, damages their personality and makes it difficult for them to take up any future work opportunities that may arise.'[4]

'Their feeling of being useless and superfluous . . . and the endlessly frustrating round of looking for work . . . give an overwhelming feeling of having been born one too many.'[5]

This dependence also extends its effects to negation of affectivity. Stable pair-bonding is impossible because they have no possibility of forming their own households. They know the effects of unemployment and consequent need from their own families and have no desire to reproduce this situation. But once they reach a certain age, the need to find a partner and set up a home becomes stronger, and they come together 'anyhow', which usually means lodging in the homes of one set of parents, with no stable income, but living off what they can scrape together, thereby reproducing the situation they had hitherto avoided, with the resultant emotional stresses that such a situation brings.

Their possibilities for affective, sexual satisfaction, on both physical and emotional planes, are frustrated, their basic vehicles for pleasure and relaxation thwarted; they find it impossible to adopt alternative roles to their parents; they cannot achieve anything intrinsically valuable; the contradiction between their ideals and reality becomes ever greater and their aspirations gradually lose all meaning. 'Work, the means of expression and personal and social bonding . . . does not exist.'[6] Furthermore, young people often have a double experience of being out of work: they themselves have none, and they are members of a family all of whom have none, which produces serious problems of family communication and integration, owing to the loss of the traditional role of the head of the family as breadwinner, which can give rise to violent behaviour and family break-up. 'The change of roles, with the comcomitant feeling of inferiority this produces for the man, and the ambivalence and confusion it produces in the woman, loads the relationship with unexpressed tensions and feelings which are generally translated into hostility and alienation.'[7]

Women adapt better to this situation, since they can continue to carry out the tasks traditionally allotted to them, but in a male-dominated culture like that of Latin America, men, if they have no work, have nothing to do.

'Estimates . . . give the young worker 1293 hours of leisure *per annum*, and 2340 hours for the young person out of work, looking for work or doing nothing.'[8] For many young people, the solution to this state of affairs is simply to run away from it. 'The thing is to make the time pass quicker than it does . . . You go anywhere there's something going on that stops you from thinking . . . thinking's the same as despairing, it's the worst thing for you. Lots of people end up on drink or grass to stop themselves thinking.'[9]

Although there are no specialised studies to go by, it is fair to deduce that the great increase in drink and drug abuse noticeable among the young is very largely due to the generalised poverty generated by lack of work. This is particularly true of the glue-sniffers, who generally come from drifting families with no settled work.

The same situation has also produced an alarming rise in the number of offences committed by minors and young people. In Santiago in 1981, a total of 211,547 people were arrested, of which 108,270, that is over half, were aged between 16 and 29. In the 16–17 age group, the commonest offences were drugs, larceny, theft and drunkenness; in the 18–19 age group, drunkenness, theft, drugs; in the 20–29 group, drunkenness and disorderly conduct, assault, theft and drugs.

These figures leave out of account one problem which is on the increase: the prostitution to which girls and young women are obliged to resort in order to survive. The problem is the more serious in that it is hard to detect, since there are now many activities which act as a cover-up for the practice of prostitution: topless bars, massage parlours, etc., in which under-age girls can work with permission from their parents or guardians.

3. ALTERNATIVES

What alternatives, what possibilities do these young people have? Some seek a solution by getting into the 'black' work sector—street vending, car minding, etc.—which is one of the sectors on which the clamp-down has been most severe. Others find a way out in the youth-training programmes organised by the government. But access to these is limited compared to the numbers eligible, with preference given to the over eighteens and particularly to those who are married.

Even those who succeed in finding work are still in a very precarious situation, since minors can by law be paid only a maximum of 60 per cent of the minimum legal wage, generally have no legal recourse against dismissal, etc.

4. UNDERSTANDING AND UNEMPLOYMENT

An experiment in setting-up training workshops in Puente Alto[10] showed that young people had no real understanding of the true causes of unemployment, but tended to associate it above all with external causes (world recession), and seeing the way out of it only in individual terms, thereby making it a problem to be overcome only on the personal level, not through collective or group effort. This situation is exacerbated by the consumerist and hedonistic culture upheld by the regime, which means that an individualistic perception of problems is not confined to young people out of work, but to young people in general and the rest of society. This makes any attempt at organising more difficult and factionalises any youth movement that might come into existence (though it is effectively non-existent at present) in advance. 'Young people feel little identification with youth; there is no such thing as a youthful understanding which identifies young people as something different from the rest, from workers or their parents . . . "Youth" is a myth.'[11]

Many young people have shut the door on the future, seeking release from their frustrations in drink and drugs. Others try to survive through recourse to prostitution or delinquency, with the consequent alienation from society that these activities suppose. So being out of work has a doubly destructive effect on young people, since 'it corrupts not only by stimulating them to crime, escapism and prostitution, but also—since it destroys their creative capabilities—by depriving them of the identity which enables them to place themselves in relation to the future'.[12]

Translated by Paul Burns

Notes

1. A. Gaete SJ in *Mensaje* 327 (Mar–Apr. 1984).

2. See Foxley-Raczynski 'Grupos vulnerables en situaciones recesivas', a study of children and young people in Chile, 1983; CODEJU-SERPAJ 'Juventud chilena: identidad y alternativas', 1982; SUR Studies 'Empleo y desempleo en la juventud' in *Juventud* Bulletin no. 2, Aug. 1983.

3. I. Agurto, and G. de la Maza 'La juventud popular: elementos para comprenderla' in *Educación y Solidaridad* 6, pub. by ECO.

4. National Commisison for Pastoral Care of Young People of the Chilean Episcopal Conference 'Antecedentes para la comprensión de la realidad de los jóvenes chilenos', 1983.

5. J. García-Huidobro and J. E. Weinstein 'Diez Entrevistas sobre la juventud chilena actual', CIDE working paper no. 10, 1980.

6. E. Lira, E. Weinstein 'La cesantía y sus efectos psicosociales' (Duplicated).

7. *Ibid.*

8. Santiago Vicariate for Pastoral Care of Young People 'Diagnóstico de la realidad juvenil en la Arquidiócesis de Santiago', 1983.

9. A. Gaete SJ, the article cited in note 1.

10. M. Cerri and E. Neumann 'El desarrollo juvenil en condiciones de marginalidad', CIDE working document no. 20, 1983.

11. García-Huidobro and Weinstein, the paper cited in note 5.

12. National Commission . . . , the report cited in note 4.

PART III

The Meaning Dimension

Miklós Tomka

Youth Malaise and Religion: the Case of Hungary

'THE EMPLOYMENT situation of young people is being marked in the eighties by more frequent and sharper conflicts. In consequence, a significant proportion of young people are left with no prospects for the future. This has far-reaching consequences for the attitudes, life-style and political outlook of young people' (from a summary of a comprehensive study of Hungarian youth).[1]

A press report of a conference of youth organisations from European socialist countries, Cuba and the Mongolian People's Republic which devoted more attention to another aspect will certainly have had included Hungary in its mind as well:

> In many socialist countries interest in religion among young people has increased, but the ideological content of this religious feeling differs from that of the past. Significant ideals which provide a basis for communal action—for example in relation to peace and the building of a socialist society—are also present in the consciousness of religious young people.[2]

The two observations are of unequal value. The phenomena in question are not equally visible, and, more important, both the problems and unease of young people and the assumed growth in religious interest are both far too complex to be described in a short quotation. Nor can their full scope be presented in an article. Nevertheless listing well-known examples can be useful; the search for causes and effects can become the road to a solution of the problem.

It is important to remember that a study of young people in Hungary cannot be taken as applicable to other socialist countries. On the contrary, Hungary is a very special case. The economic growth of the 1970s is often described as 'the Hungarian economic miracle', and political stability and increased opportunities for personal development go hand in hand. Accordingly, any search for common factors, such as social mobility in the socialist countries—high for two decades, but in rapid decline during the last ten years—must be based on an awareness of the particular situation of each country.

In the social context with which we are concerned 'youth' is an elusive concept. Many experts deny the existence of such a stage as 'youth'. Official Hungarian usage defines it as the period between the ages of 14 and 30 or 35. For our purposes, however it is enough to regard 'youth' as the transitional stage, the stage of life and social role in which a person becomes autonomous and adult. Attaining autonomy includes finding a job, with the resulting social status and income, building up a life and household of one's own and the creation, acceptance or choice of the human and social ties appropriate for the person and his or her social characteristics. The acquisition of independence thus has important physical and material as well as formal structural aspects. Under growth to adulthood come elements of outlook and responsibility. Becoming adult involves a choice of aims in life, the conscious acceptance of a scale of values, the building of a personal identity. The person's status in social and material life, and their position in relation to cosmic or transcendental questions, are also involved in this process as matter for reflection.

1. THREE SIGNS OF ADULTHOOD

The concepts or ideas of winning independence and becoming adult have a further quality: they set up relations. They are related to a norm of independence and adulthood which has become established through history and culture. In a specific case it is only in relation to this standard—which is different in each situation—that there can be talk of the level of achievement or of success or failure. The norm itself is defined implicitly in lengthy socio-historical processes. It is approximately embodied in the level of independence reached by preceding generations (perhaps slightly modified by contact with other ways of life in other societies).

(a) A job

The first step on the road to independence is a job. There is no unemployment in Hungary, though people find difficulty in getting a job to match their educational qualifications or near home. In the competition for better paid and more prestigious positions, or for local jobs, young people are at a disadvantage. Despite a continuing explosion in education, (in 1980 36 per cent of the working population below the age of 30 had the senior school-leaving certificate, but only 19 per cent of older people), the proportion of young people in white-collar jobs is falling, from 34 per cent to 29 per cent in the period 1970–80.[3] Young academics must increasingly accept non-academic jobs, and skilled workers are finding that the only openings available are in unskilled posts. Commuting is a burden which falls most heavily on young people. Twenty per cent of all employees, 37 per cent of 25–29 year olds, 42 per cent of 19–24 year olds and as many as 48 per cent of under-18s work outside their own area.[4] Of course, it may be assumed that young people are not always forced to travel, but motivated by higher earnings. Nevertheless greater effort and a search for better paid jobs do not always lead to the expected success. 'A higher qualification less and less frequently guarantees a higher income. The gap between the earnings level of those entering employment and average earnings, or the time taken for first-time workers to reach the average, is greater the higher the level of education of the young worker at the time of starting work. The general picture, which emerges clearly from research and statistics, is that the principle of rumuneration which, while differing according to performance, rewards qualifications no longer applies to young people.'[5] Seniority has now become the criterion for promotion, with the result that there are very few young people in senior positions or among high earners. Their problem is the result, not so much of this enforced delay, as of the reduction in mobility. The political upheaval of the late 1940s and 1950s, together with the expansion of industry and the service sector in the 1950s and 1960s, created countless new jobs and filled them with—at the time—young people. The end of large-scale economic development is equivalent, with existing promotion policies, to a sentence which requires young people to spend the first two to three years of their working lives in subordinate and worse paid positions. The worsening in the relative earnings of young people can be documented since the beginning to middle of the 1960s. In the period 1962–77 the average basic earnings of 35–39 year olds rose by 227 per cent, and that of under 35 year olds by only 204 per cent. Young people received only 90 per cent of the increase received by their elders.[6] Whether this change brought about an increase or a decrease in the real income of young people is hard to determine. Our intention here is to indicate 'discrimination' against young people, and some of the roots of confrontation between young people and the older generation.

A comparison of earnings is, however, deceptive. In a society in which almost all women work (and have to, for financial reasons), the period of setting up a household, the birth and education of children, is an extremely difficult stage of life. After childbirth mothers have a right to five months' leave on full pay. If a women wishes to stay at home longer, she may do so up to the end of the child's third year and receive a lump sum, which at present is equal to about 20–25 per cent of average earnings. Consequently it is not just the reduction in a wife's earnings which creates problems for family budgets, but the expense of children. In families with two or more children per capita income, which naturally depends on the number of children, amounts to between 48 per cent and 79 per cent of that of families without children. The attainment of financial independence is such a slow and uncertain process that in most cases people do not make it a precondition of marriage. (In the capital, however, young people are reacting to the particularly difficult income and housing conditions by postponing marriage.) Marriage brings a new trap. If the couple want to be materially independent, self-sufficient, adult in this sense, the clever thing to do is to have no children or a limited number. However, this threatens personal maturation and the development of responsibility. This is a less obvious result. The rational decision made by many young couples in Hungary is not to have children, or to have at most one or two. The resulting ageing of the population displaces the social consequences by a few decades, to a period in which it is not today's older generation, but today's young people, who will in the meantime have become old, will be affected. Today's young people have not succeeded in shaking off the burden imposed on them, but have at most distributed it better.

(b) A home of one's own

A further element, and probably the most important obstacle for young people in building a life of their own, is the housing shortage. Rented rooms cost, per person, 50 per cent–120 per cent of the average earnings of a person entering employment. The landlords often forbid visits from members of the opposite sex (even a husband or wife). If a couple find a room, 'no pregnancies' is often a condition of the tenancy. Other possibilities are buying a home, building one or applying for a State allocation. The purchase prices of 60 sq m. flats are about twice to two-and-a-half times average earnings, a sum totally beyond the reach of young people. Even much more modest solutions absorb the earnings of both partners. Husbands are under particular pressure to sacrifice their leisure time, and to do a second job at the end of work at their main place of employment, and frequently also on Saturdays and Sundays. In the case of older people this 'work addiction' may be a sign of uncontrolled consumerism, but for young people it is the only way to anything like an independent life.

A common way of getting a home is building for oneself, with the help of relatives, colleagues and friends. Obtaining the materials, the work itself and paying the help take a full five to eight years. Flats allocated by the State cost about 20–30 months' income, but applications can in practice only be made after marriage, and there is an average wait of six to eight years. (In the case of self-built houses, there are loans to be paid off, and if a flat is allocated by the State there is a rent. Whatever the arrangement, once a home is acquired it absorbs a monthly sum equivalent to around 25 per cent of a young person's average earnings. In the case of self-build houses payments run for fifteen years; with State accommodation they continue indefinitely.) For want of a home of their own, almost two-thirds of young married couples live with parents. In the more fortunate cases couples can live together, but often they cannot. In addition to the financial dependence resulting from the need to devote all their efforts to acquiring a home, this brings personal dependence on parents. The result is that it is almost impossible to make an attempt at material or personal independence before the age of twenty-five. It is hard to decide whether to regard this as a prolongation of the stage of youth or to criticise this version of youth as such, particularly since it is only partly devoted to the creation of space and independence and largely to forced acceptance of a disadvantaged position, with fewer possibilities of independence than even the previous generation had and have. In this extended phase responsibilities and roles are unclear. Young people must simultaneously play many roles, which can only be combined with immense difficulty. They must simultaneously live up to adult norms and the corresponding expectations among young people. From the age of eighteen young people are treated as full citizens, with the right to vote, but the problems surrounding starting work and the search for a place to live remind them, day in day out, of the hard facts of their many-sided dependence.[7]

2. DISTURBED SOCIALISATION

For a sixth of children the cutting of links with the family begins at six months, for another two-thirds at the age of three, when they are taken into a crêche or nursery. Hungarians are now in educational institutions—and in peer groups—from their earliest years. Both situations, however, create little security or capacity for love. As a result (although the real causes may lie deeper and earlier), a sense of sociability is lacking. Friendships and social relationships become rare commodities. More and more young people are rejecting a life-time commitment in marriage. The divorce rate has been increasing continuously since 1960; it has tripled in the last twenty years. In almost a third of divorces in Hungary in 1982 both partners were below the age of thirty. Not only personal relationships are weak; young people are increasingly reluctant to join clubs or youth organisations.

There is no need to give further evidence that this state of affairs and this behaviour shapes the outlook of young people. Semi-official studies comment that 'Young people have every reason to feel betrayed and sold out . . . and to see no future.'[8] A growing mistrust of official institutions and organisations is a natural result. 'For more and more young people, the distance between their outlook, problems, life-style, behaviour and goals and the existing social and political situation, or their perception of it, can be measured in light years.'[9] The general reaction, however, is not opposition, but a sense of powerlessness and a withdrawal into a private world.[10] Another is deviant behaviour: a growth in juvenile crime, alcoholism and (less frequently) drugs. This variant frequently leads to its logical conclusion. The suicide rate among the 15–39 age group rose by 40 per cent between 1960 and 1980. In the 20–29 age group suicide is the main cause of death. Twenty-eight per cent of male deaths and 20 per cent of female deaths in this age group were suicides.[11]

Disturbed socialisation and the lack of community ties are sufficient, even without socio-economic problems, to produce a crisis of values. This destroys individual as well as social identity. The older generations found their place in life and their identity in a different historical situation, and in this respect the younger generation is in a very difficult position. Asserting their identity materially and psychologically is a laborious task which faces many obstacles. They feel that their attempts to play a part in shaping society have failed. The more intimate communities which should provide refuge—friends, family, etc.—are proving, under the pressure of day-to-day problems and a deep-rooted egoism, to be far too fragile. Finally, the overwhelming majority of Hungary's young people, despite a general hunger for religion, have nowhere to satisfy their cosmic or transcendental dimension.

These are the symptoms, but the diagnosis is only complete when the causes are uncovered. The facts can be interpreted either as a 'class struggle' between the generations,[12] or as evidence of increasing individualism. In both cases the social system is seriously threatened. The social underpinning of people's capacity to survive is being reduced to the provision of the bare minimum of material and organisational support. (There is no need to stress that the first to suffer from this are young people.) This raises the question why a society which quite recently functioned well could become so weak despite (or because of?) economic growth, political stability and freedom of expression. Among the causes is the undermining of the institutions of socialisation. The family was the main victim of the enormous mobility of the post-war period. Many of today's young people grew up without siblings, with only one parent or in State institutions. The family has also lost its role through the provision of State institutions to relieve working mothers: crêches, residential nurseries, day-nurseries, boarding schools, etc. The older generation tolerates and allows this 'theft' of children even though it has long since become clear that schools and institutions are failing in the central tasks of education, the transmission of values, the communication of ideals, the preparation of young people for autonomous human existence. Young people are thus the victims of their parents' individualism. Neighbourhood and family ties fragmented by social mobility also cannot play their part in socialisation and the creation of social stability. Among the few institutions which remain are the churches, although in practice, in order to purchase their freedom to run impersonal liturgical activity, they have abandoned organisations and community life, cultural and community-building roles. In so doing they have taken their place among the official organisations of society which young people are now rejecting and which have become insignificant in the production and reproduction of culture and the social system.

3. YOUTH AND RELIGION

In 1975 or 1980 this report would have to have ended here, with the following implicit conclusions: (a) Hungarian society is in numerical decline; (b) the social system is progressively collapsing; (c) religion has lost its social relevance and may be disappearing; (d) these tendencies affect generations unequally, with the main impact falling on young people. (To put it bluntly, to the extent that young people want to reach the material level of their parents, they are in serious danger of losing all personal and social security. It is ironic that even so equality in possessions and income is not guaranteed. In contrast to previous generations, young people now are recognising this dilemma and having to deal with it in the form of an individual choice.)

In contrast to previous periods, there are now signs among young people which may point to a change. Forecasts continue to predict population decline. In addition, the fundamental difference and separateness between the personal and community and the institutional and organisational spheres of society has recently come to be widely noted—a situation which perhaps has similarities with Western societies.[13] Hope for the rebuilding of community structures is now based on experience with young people. As a reaction to the lack of social protection, or simply as a way or consequence of discovering identity, youth groups are forming around particular crystallisation points, such as music, sport, deviance, politics, religion.[14] For the reasons mentioned above, most of these groups are short-lived, but at least the religious small groups or basic communities seem to be more solid. Their numbers, which run into the thousands, their durability—many by now have lasted more than a decade—and their contribution to shaping religious life and everyday life seem to offer hope for the future. Firstly, they seem to be a means of breaking through the alienation of the Christian tradition and the Church and halting the trend to dechristianisation.[15] One urban study found that 16 per cent of believing and practising young people had had no religious upbringing. For them the way to Christianity and the closest social embodiment of it is the small religious group. Secondly, their example is also attracting attention in secular life, as they offer social sensitivity and commitment as an alternative to the general stress on privacy. In an atmosphere of weariness with ideology they maintain firm convictions, they confront growing amorality, particularly in public life and work, with their firm ethical position, and naturally, in contrast to the atomisation and individualisation of society they display the possibility of community ties.

Religious interest among young people, limited though it may be, may point to one way in which young people can cope with their problems—even in Hungary. The report quoted at the beginning of this article indicates that similar ideas are being entertained elsewhere.

Translated by Francis McDonagh

Notes

1. J. Andics 'A fiatal nemzedék társadalmi-foglalkozási helyzetéről és perspektíváiról' (On the social and employment position and prospects of the young generation), *Ifjúsági Szemle* 4 (1983) 17–26.

2. Report from MTI, the Hungarian press agency, in the Hungarian Socialist Workers' Party daily, *Népszabadság*, 26 Oct 1984, 4.

3. *A magyar ifjúság a nyolcvanas években* (Hungary's Youth in the 1980s) (Budapest 1983) p. 31.

4. Andics, the article cited in note 1, p. 19.

5. *A magyar ifjúság*, the work cited in note 3, p. 23.

6. *Ibid.* p. 248.

7. *Ibid.* p. 186.

8. *Ibid.* pp. 20–21.

9. *Ibid.* p. 187.

10. *Ibid.* p. 196; and M. Tomka 'Jugend in Ungarn' *Europäische Rundschau* 4 (1983) pp. 135–141.

11. *A magyar ifjúság*, the work cited in note 3, p. 92.

12. Gerhard Lenski *Power and Privilege* (New York 1966).

13. James S. Coleman *Power and the Structure of Society* (New York 1974).

14. *A magyar ifjuság*, the work cited in note 3, pp. 183 and 199.

15. At present 54 per cent of Hungarians describe themselves as religious, but this self-assessment is in inverse proportion to age. Up to five or ten years ago young people were the least religious group in Hungarian society (see M. Tomka 'The Religious— Non-religious Dichotomy as a Social Problem' *The Annual Review of the Social Sciences of Religion* 3 (1979) 105–137). Today, in addition to the intelligentsia, young people in particular show signs of a religious revival, which is leading to a measurable increase in religious activity among young people. On the other hand, for a correct evaluation of these findings it is important to note that only about 3 per cent of young people attend religious services on Sunday and that the Church reaches less than 1 per cent of young people between the ages of 14 and 25 with any kind of catechesis, religious education or further education. This statistic does not include the independent religious youth groups, which meet off church premises. The presence of Christian models of life they succeed in maintaining among young people is probably more significant than their numerical strength.

Eileen Barker

'And so to bed':
Protest and Malaise among Youth in
Great Britain

DAMIAN SAYS cheerfully, 'It's all downhill after you're eighteen'—so he's reached the peak . . . It's two o'clock and the sun is shining. Darren, who has been up for half an hour, says he thinks his generation is apathetic. 'There aren't any young action groups. They're all in bed, I suppose, like everybody else.'

(The *Observer*, 25 November 1984)

The sub-title of my essay was suggested by the editors of this volume. At first glance it might seem as though 'Malaise and Protest . . .' would be a more logical order, but in fact some sort of protest among Britain's youth was evident for about three decades before the current malaise of chronic unemployment was to manifest itself. Had Damian been able to observe the protesting youth of his parents' generation, he might well have concluded that the world is your oyster once you're eighteen.

The youth cultures which were to become the vehicle for protest first became visible in Britain in the 1950s. The country had recovered from the immediate aftermath of the War and was enjoying an economic boom. There emerged a generation of young people who, whilst not yet burdened with mortgages or parenthood, had well-paid jobs which allowed them considerable spending power and leisure time. In 1960, the abolition of National Service ended an enforced two years of strict regimentation for male school-leavers; the 1960s also saw the widespread introduction of 'the pill'.

Youth was, it seemed, liberated from the constraints of childhood and as yet unencumbered with the responsibilities of adulthood. A hitherto uninterrupted transition from childhood to adulthood had become characterised by a period during which young people defined themselves, and were defined by the rest of the population, as sharing a discrete cultural identity. Through their music, clothes and hairstyles (and, in some cases, their motor bikes) the groups were distinguishable, not just as sub-cultures, but also as counter-cultures that questioned and rejected the values and attitudes of their elders.

It did not take long for youth to become the pampered customer of numerous commercial enterprises which were exclusively geared towards catering for (and, indeed, creating) this new market; the media also played an important role in advertising and defining the image of youth. It is impossible to estimate the membership of any of the groups, but, despite sensationalist reports in the press, none of them ever reached anything like the proportions of a mass protest movement. Nevertheless, the groups undoubtedly reflected and affected the attitudes of a far greater number of young people than those most immediately involved.

1. MIDDLE-CLASS VS. WORKING CLASS YOUTH

It has already been intimated that youth protest in Britain has appeared in a number of different guises. There have, for instance, been quite strong divisions between middle-class and working-class groups, and within both classes protest has been both radical and reactionary. For some, the past was a golden age and protest was directed for changing standards and/or changing conditions of housing or employment, or the break-up of urban communities. For others, the trouble was defined as the oppression of structures and/or of those in power and thus, it was declared, nothing but radical change could advance the world in an acceptable direction.

Middle-class youth protest in Britain has been fairly closely allied to that in North America and other parts of Europe. It was, perhaps, first identifiable as part of the Campaign for Nuclear Disarmament (CND), then, during the 1960s, it took the form of student demonstrations and virulent attacks upon the 'bourgeois, capitalist imperialism of the West'. There being no notable success in changing the structure of society, the next stage was the hippy rejection of *all* structures in favour of the loving anarchy of 'flower-power'. This did not last much longer, however—partly because antinomianism can rapidly turn into anomie, and partly because the economic (and political) climate became less conducive to the luxury of rejection. 'Drop-outs' began to drop back into the system, although some would continue the self-liberation that the hippies had advocated by joining 'human potential' groups in which they learned to meditate or explore their inner psyches, while upholding capitalism with sufficient diligence to enable them to pay for the liberating courses they pursued. Others continued to protest, but, as a reaction to the permissiveness and/or secularity of the age, they would join a charismatic group, a 'House Church', or, occasionally, one of the more authoritarian of the new religious movements. More recently there has been a resurgence of interest in the Peace Movement, evidenced to some degree by the support given to a group of women camping outside the Cruise missile base at Greenham Common.

Working-class protest groups in Britain have been less obviously part of a North American trend, or, when their counterparts have been found elsewhere, it has been more likely (as with the Beatles or punk) that the craze originated in Britain. The appearance of the 'teddy boys' (who dressed in the style of young men in the reign of Edward VII) was the first obvious sign that working class youth had acquired a sub-culture of its own. The teds rejected the values of both the middle classes and their elders, but they did not confine their protest to the cultural symbols of their clothes or their rock 'n' roll music; many of them were actively involved in assaults upon the Black population, which was blamed for all manner of ills besetting the working classes. As with other working-class groups which have seen it as their moral duty to resort to violence, membership tended to be almost exclusively male—female followers being tolerated merely for the services they could supply to enhance the macho image.

The boom in conspicuous leisure consumption, coupled with sensationalist reporting by the media, was continued by two rival groups, the mods and rockers, during the 1960s, and, in the 1970s, by the skinheads, whose protest took the form of attacking categories of persons (such as Pakistanis, hippies and homosexuals) whom they considered to be threatening their traditional way of life. Young Blacks (most of whom had been born after their parents had emigrated from the West Indies), were no longer a primary target for attack by white youth, but they have probably encountered greater obstacles in their education, housing and employment than any other section of British society since the War. Around the mid-1970s, the Rastafarian movement provided the Blacks with a forum for protest, then the rastas' reggae music provided one of the bases from which there emerged the most vocal manifestation of youth protest against *everything* which British society may have held dear. Punks, with crops of exotic pink and/or green hair sticking, cockatoo fashion, out of heads adorned with safety pins, exulted in exuding not only foul language, but spit and vomit from their black-painted mouths.

Both the rastas and the punks articulated bitterness and resentment against the society in which they lived, but while the former were offered, through the religious tenets of Rastafarianism, a sense of meaning in history and the promise that a better future awaited them, the punks enjoyed no such hopes. There was, nevertheless, some sense of identity and comradeship to be found in membership of so vivid a protest group.

2. FROM PROTEST TO APATHY

It is notoriously difficult to detect trends at the time that they are occurring, but it does seem that, although punks, skins, mods and other youth types are still to be found, an unusually subdued atmosphere has descended upon British youth. It is as though the boisterous forms of protest of the past were no longer any fun. Sporadic outbreaks of violence erupted in the streets of a number of urban centres in 1981, and there continues to be a certain amount of football hooliganism, but protest *as a sub-culture* appears to have given way to a new sense of apathy. Instead of reject*ing*; youth finds itself reject*ed*.

Over 13 per cent of the British workforce (some three and a quarter million people) were unemployed as 1984 drew to a close. The rates are much worse in some areas (20 per cent in Northern Ireland, 18 per cent in the North of England), and much, much worse for school-leavers, particularly if they happen to be Black. The rate of unemployment for people who are aged 25 or over is approximately 10 per cent, but about 28 per cent for teenagers. Young people under the age of 25 account for just under one third of all those unemployed for a year or more. The official figures for October 1984 show the size of the problem in absolute numbers:

Time unemployed	Age			
	Under 18	*18 yrs*	*19 yrs*	*20–24*
up to 26 weeks	192,175	115,543	87,297	324,438
26–52 weeks	24,919	31,715	28,587	115,466
53–104 weeks	16,862	38,711	41.493	107,560
over 104 weeks	7	9,656	21,848	130,082
Total	233,963	195,625	179,225	677,546

The extent to which this particular malaise is a comparatively recent phenomenon is illustrated by the fact that, in 1978, 88 per cent (402,000 out of 456,000) school-leavers were employed on leaving school; in 1983, the figure was 38 per cent (166,000 out of 433,000). At a time when there were over 600,000 unemployed teenagers in the United Kingdom (excluding the 300,000 in the Youth Training Scheme), there were less than a thousand 'real job' vacancies noted at career offices for young people.

In the modern Welfare State, it is certainly true that, although *subjectively* one may feel deprived of material comforts, the vast majority of people do not face starvation; they can secure shelter from the elements and, in most cases, can enjoy protection from physical attack by their fellow citizens. The State *provides* its members with a substantial minumum. What the State does not always provide, however, is an opportunity for its members to *contribute*. Being in a position in which one is forced to take more than one can give may seem, on the face of it, to be a cushy deal, but in fact it is probably one of the most dispiriting and humiliating situations that a person can face. One does not have to be a Marxist to accept that a philosophical anthropology which starts from a view of humankind as *Homo Faber* can alert us to some fundamentally important truths about the need for people to play a creative role in the society of which they are a part.

One must not exaggerate the situation. The majority of people do find some sort of employment. But many face reduced prospects of security of tenure or of promotion (as others, senior to them, are increasingly unlikely to move on). Bright students who are among those with the highest chances of a promising career have told me that they had planned to take a year out either before going to university or after graduating, but they no longer dared risk letting their peers get ahead of them now that the pressure for jobs is so great. Even those who are in relatively secure occupations admit to a cloud hanging over their future prospects—as one young accountant said 'I'm doing quite well at the moment, but I know damn well that eventually accountancy too will suffer, because everything gets affected in a situation like this'.

But these are people who are still looking ahead. It is possible to argue that both prosperity and unemployment have contributed to an erosion of any concept of deferred gratification among the young. First, in a period of prosperity, the future could seem sufficiently secure to look after itself. Hire-purchase companies freely encouraged a 'live now—pay later' attitude. At the same time, there were some areas in which the expanding economy did promote a future orientation. Education was one instance. The more paper qualifications one could acquire, and the higher the grades on these bits of paper, the more likelihood there was of getting a good job. With the coming of high unemployment, however, the bits of paper, while still necessary, no longer guaranteed work. More and more young people who previously might have seen some point in studying are now convinced that formal learning is utterly irrelevant to their futures. This has resulted not only in their playing truant whenever possible and leaving school as soon as they reach the minimum age of sixteen, but also in the spreading of an attitude which does little to promote the idea that their future can be improved by anything they do now. This attitude is further reinforced by young people's lack of confidence in there being *any* future for them. Other contributors to this volume will explore the effect of the threat of nuclear disaster upon young people, but I should like to record that when I asked a group of just over a hundred young Britons to describe what they thought the world would look like in the year 2000, a significant number indicated that they did not believe that there would *be* a year 2000. Many others were highly sceptical about the quality of life that they could expect—at individual, national or international levels. Not only do young people feel that they have very little control over their lives in the modern world of structured unemployment, inhuman bureaucracies, and multi-national corporations, but they also feel that those whom they might have expected to have some power (teachers, politicians, clergy, employers) are themselves unable to control the forces that are pushing us hither and thither. For some young people it is the Thatcher government which is, directly or indirectly, responsible for their insecurity, for others it is the Americans and/or the Russians, but for the majority it is a nebulous, undefined 'them'. Whoever it is, there is little or nothing that the young people themselves can do about it. They might as well eat, drink and be merry on the day they collect their dole—otherwise, why bother to get out of bed?

3. PARTICIPATION AND A SENSE OF PURPOSE

Furthermore, despite the fact that their *basic* needs are met by the welfare State, a less fundamental, but none the less very real, form of identity crisis has arisen for young people through their inability to consume—in the manner to which they had become accustomed. I have already mentioned the increased spending power which Western youth enjoyed during the 'never-had-it-so-good' years. Many young people, especially those in the working classes, had begun to identify their peers and themselves through their consumption patterns. They became what they bought, rather that what they produced. In such a context, when one has no work, one is in danger of finding oneself without the wherewithal to purchase one's identity. One response has been, quite simply, to steal one's identity. More petty theft is committed by children (particularly boys) than by any other section of British society. The prospect of a short prison sentence is not much of a deterrent to those who feel that the alternatives are not much better. Other responses have been hardly more reassuring. The perfectly healthy, if somewhat irritating, exuberance to be found in the protest groups of the sixties and seventies seems to have been cowed, but where protest is visible it erupts as mindless violence in the form of street riots, 'Paki-bashing' or football hooliganism. More frequently, however, the response has been a withdrawal from any kind of outwardly directed activity; sometimes, with tragic consequences, it has been an escape to alcohol, drugs or the less expensive habit of glue-sniffing.

Young people are extremely adaptable, but adaptation can be with apathy and resignation to hopelessness, helplessness and worthlessness. The next generation of adults may well be highly skilled in the ability to survive by drifting, with passive endurance, through a life without targets or goals. But, surely, there must be some things which can enable young people to feel that it is worth getting out of bed and not going to prison?

Some time ago, I distributed a questionnaire to young people in which I asked them to describe what they had done and how they had felt the previous day. For many the day had seemed boring and aimless, but this did not apply to those respondents who, elsewhere in the questionnaire, had confessed to some kind of faith or who belonged to a religious organisation. It seemed as though religion was sufficient to give some sort of meaning to daily life, although it certainly was not the only source of meaningfulness—marriage, friendships, work, politics, music or a commitment to helping others could also make the day (and the respondent) seem worthwhile. Much has been written about the spiritual poverty which pervades modern society, but it is difficult to assess the extent to which young people are in fact spiritually impoverished. It is certainly true that very large numbers reject any kind of organised religion. The Church is frequently labelled hypocritical, apathetic or irrelevant, and clergy are accused of being either so remote or so trendy that any serious discussion with them is impossible. This does not mean, however, that young people do not have a yearning to explore questions of a religious and/or spiritual nature. More than one study has shown that an unexpectedly large proportion of young people have had some kind of religious or spiritual experience which they have never discussed with anyone. It seems as though neither the concepts nor a context conducive to exploring questions of meaning, identity, belonging and self-worth are readily available to young people. Of course, these opportunities are available in some families, some schools and some churches; there are schemes which give young people the chance to help others and, thereby, to give their own lives a meaning and a purpose; there *are* ways of helping young people to feel that they want to get out of bed in the morning and that, even if they have just received their fiftieth rejection slip, there could still be a worthwhile way of spending their day. But Damian and his friends are going to need a lot of help if it's not going to be all downhill now they are eighteen.

PART IV

The Apocalyptic Dimension

Michael Warren

Young People and the Nuclear Threat

CONSIDER THE significance for youth today of the following facts reported by a group of scientists in the mid-1980s:

'American and Soviet arsenals contain about 18,000 strategic thermonuclear warheads, with a ... yield of 10,000 megatons [about 500,000 Hiroshimas], in addition to about 35,000 tactical and intermediate weapons. Yet not more than 500 to 2,000 strategic warheads would be enough to trigger a climatic catastrophe threatening the survival of the human race.'[1]

According to these calculations based on commonly known data, the world could have had one Hiroshima-sized blast every day starting in 1945 and could continue doing so for far more than fifteen hundred years.

Obviously these astonishing facts have immense consequences for the youngest in the human family, whose futures are put in ever greater jeopardy the farther we move from the carefully justified misjudgment of August 1945. Are young people aware of these dangers? At what ages do they become capable of being aware and at what levels of awareness? What are the effects of their awareness? What should the churches be doing in pastoral work with the young people in the face of these issues? These important questions will not be easily faced or answered by those seeking fidelity to youth in the name of the Gospel.

Faithfulness in our day to both the human family and the community of followers of Jesus demands a keen kind of perceptual courage needed to stare long and hard at social evil and to discern its implications for action.[2] Fidelity in our time will mean for some the descent into hell, that is, an unflinching look at evil actual and potential in our world, a look that can only bring one to the end of one's resources and to echo the anguished cry of the condemned in Elie Weisel's *Night*: 'Where is God?' Many who work with youth are not ready for this sort of perceptual courage.

If the questions listed above will not be easily faced, then neither will they be easily answered. For forty years adults have colluded in avoiding the work needed to answer these questions. If anything, as destructiveness of the weapons has increased over the years along with the volume of information about the consequences of even accidental detonation, so has the seriousness of the moral lapse in the silence and inactivity of adults. One researcher makes the following accusation:

'The fact that there is so little information available about how young people feel about nuclear issues that affect their lives so vitally suggests that we adults have entered into a kind of compact with ourselves not to know. We suspect that the implications of what we are doing to the emotional development of our young are so horrifying that we would prefer to remain ignorant, for the veil of denial is easy enough to tear away once we set out to do so.'[3]

There have, however, been a small group of researchers who have been quietly studying these questions and whose pioneering work eventually opened the way for a wider and more intense study of them starting about 1977.

1. OUR SCIENTIFIC KNOWLEDGE

One of the earliest studies, Sybelle Escalona's 'Children and the Threat of Nuclear War', is still cited often for its special insights.[4] After studying children's reactions to the 1962 Cuban Missile Crisis, she concluded that children apparently know 'a great deal more than we sometimes give them credit for. Children seem so absorbed in their games, their friends, their life at school, that it is hard to believe they pay much attention to grown-up problems. *Yet even young children nearly always seem to know when something really matters to their elders.* As soon as American families became concerned over issues of fallout, testing and shelter building, children also knew about these issues. Signs of their awareness turned up in the questions they asked and even in the games they played.'[5]

Escalona reported that in 1961, when nuclear testing was stirring international concern, 98 per cent of ten and eleven year old children in one New York City school showed concern that there might not be a future world for them. Based on her studies, she concluded that 'children four years old and up are aware of a danger to life. With greater or lesser understanding, they connect this danger with the language of nuclear war—fallout, Russia, radiation, H-bomb are all part of their vocabulary.'[6] Particularly valuable in Escalona's report were her suggestions for parents in helping children have a continued sense of hope in the face of apocalyptic dread.

A leitmotif threaded through Escalona's account is an assumption that a major problem for children and youth facing apocalyptic fears of destruction is the unwillingness of many parents and other adults to face these questions. In the minds of children especially, fearful matters one is not allowed to talk about are perceived to be particularly bad or frightening. Silence only exacerbates fear.[7] On the other hand children and older young people are helped simply by knowing that parents are thinking about such issues and have some definite ideas about them. Many later researchers have echoed Escalona's claim that young people draw strength from adults who do not shrink from questions troubling youth and who communicate that life and human values are worth fighting for.[8] Conclusions such as these have obvious implications for those ministering to youth who may have decided, not always with full consciousness, that songs, hugs, and allusions to a loving God will absolve young people from worry about nuclear extinction.

2. THE PROMISE OF THE FUTURE

Some claim that the single most important force helping young people in their slow struggle for maturity is the promise which the future holds, a promise that makes the process of growing up worthwhile.[9] However, when the future holds no promise but is itself perceived to be in jeopardy, youth move towards forms of despair. One psychologist describes the sequence as follows. 'There are many . . . disappointments which a child must endure, such as the realisation of being small or relatively weak, or that adult sexuality and child-bearing are beyond a small girl's reach, or simply that there are other children who are smarter, better athletes, or in some respects more lovable. In adolescence, heightened sexual feeling, a desire for independence, and the development of new skills and capabilities are accompanied by the possibility of hurt and rebuff. At each stage of development, the child mitigates disappointments by looking ahead and buiding a vision of the future in which he or she may possess what cannot now be had, or in which it is possible to become what he or she is incapable of being now . . . . But what happens to the ego ideal if society and its leaders are perceived cynically and the future itself is uncertain . . .? In such a context, impulsivity, a value system of "get it now", the hyperstimulation of drugs, and the proliferation of apocalyptic cults . . . seem to be natural developments.'[10] In spite of such descriptions of the pyschological ramifications of life in the nuclear shadow, many persons working with youth continue to claim that youth are unaffected by the problem. To an extent, this claim has some merit, as explained by Escalona in 1965: 'Many teenagers act as though they neither knew nor cared about a threat to their future. When nuclear issues are mentioned, they turn them into a joke, or pay no attention, or become impatient. Some parents are concerned not because their adolescents worry too much about the danger but rather because they seem to show callous indifference.'[11]

Researchers continue to pay close attention to the question of how and why some young people seem to be aware and to care while others do not. Perhaps the closest scrutiny of the psychological processes affected by the threat of extinction has been done by Robert Jay Lifton, who has elaborated his theory of psychic numbing, the process of becoming immune, at least on the conscious level, to matters so frightening they are more easily repressed than faced.[12] Ironically, a good summary of Lifton's later positions on this matter can be found in Escalona's early essay. She wrote: 'Whenever people deliberately close their eyes to facts, it means that they feel helpless and fatalistic. As one fifteen-year-old said, "Nothing can change things, no matter what you do." Refusal to acknowledge something unpleasant does not do away with it. Disturbing feelings still exist and undermine basic security, even when the adolescent does not admit these feelings to the self. Moreover, we know that a sense of being powerless over one's own fate is one of the most painful feelings in human experience. Somehow, the expression of unconcern and disinterest do not ring true. They mask the underlying sense of apprehension.'[13] Until recently, statements such as this have become truisms in the literature dealing with youth in face of apocalyptic destruction.

3. AN ONGOING EXPERIMENT

Many working with youth still find this description useful, but others note in it a kind of circular reasoning: some young people are consciously concerned about survival in the face of nuclear weapons; the remainder, not consciously concerned, are still vitally concerned since they have unwittingly repressed their concern in an unhealthy way. This serious objection was made by psychiatrist, Robert Coles, in 1984, in a paper challenging researchers on these questions to become more rigorous in their methods and cautioning readers of such research not to overlook the nuances and qualifications found in the best studies.[14] In the United States, for example, Coles claimed that most studies have been biased toward certain populations, such as urban and middle and upper class young people, and reflect certain social and cultural concerns of these groups.[15] Further, many studies have dealt with very small populations, from which few generalisations could be drawn. Coles' warning reminds all that study of the effects of the nuclear threat on individuals and groups of various ages is at an introductory, almost primitive stage. His caveat encourages youth ministers to keep open questions truly open and to approach their work with youth as on ongoing experiment.

Coles' reflections, however, should not intimidate those working with youth from striving to make tentative connections between the various aspects of the lives of young people and the spectre of nuclear annihilation. For example, consider the following facts about the social condition of young people in a single country. In the United States, the suicide rate for white males aged 15–19 rose between 1950 and 1978, from 6.6 per 100,000 persons to 20.8, though the rate for adults remained comparatively constant.[16]

During that same interval, the homicide rate for all youth in that age bracket doubled. It is worth noting that 1950 was the year when large numbers of children in the US began civil defence drills in schools. Between 1960 and 1972, the number of females under 18 arrested for violent crimes increased 388 per cent in the US, while the number of males arrested for these crimes rose 203 per cent.[17] In 1978, more than 22 per cent of White youth in the US aged 16–19 were victims of crimes of either violence or theft.[18] For crimes of violence alone, the victimisation rate was 73 per one thousand, or about 8 per cent. In 1982, the US Surgeon General estimated that by the age of eighteen most young people in that country would have seen about 18,000 murders enacted on television.[19]

While social science research may have difficulty establishing causal relationships among these facts, anyone concerned for youth has a right and possibly a duty to seek connections and possible explanations for them. Such demographic statistical data is available in almost all nations, and so any person concerned for youth can appropriately pay attention to these data to see if youth in their land are growing up in a culture of violence. If so, they can allow themselves to be troubled at the possible connection between the nuclear arms race and the burgeoning cloud of personal violence under which youth in many countries seem to be living.

4. SOCIAL ANALYSIS

If persons working with youth choose to deal at all with the apocalyptic threat they share with young people, they will have to search out strategies appropriate to the issue. The task of finding these strategies and of implementing them will not be an easy one. They will face the continuing problem faced by those intervening educationally in the lives of young people, namely, the submerged consciousness of youth. In childhood the process of socialisation of its very nature tends to present social reality to the child as taken-for-granted and unquestionable. Though this or that particular arrangement can and will be questioned by a child, the wider social reality is not and indeed cannot be questioned. It is a given. Instead of being seen, the social system is the lens through which one sees, and is thus invisible. In the expression, 'submerged consciousness', the metaphor suggests the fish swimming in water but unaware of the environment as water.[20] This submerged state continues into the teen years.

Thus the problem of coming to understand social reality is of its very nature complex and difficult, partly because of the nature of social structures themselves, which are both complex and not easily seen. These structures operate in the spaces between and among persons. It is one thing to describe what a person does; all one has to do is to observe the behaviour with some care. However, to get at how the social structure influences that person's behaviour one needs to know whose commands that person is following or whose norms the person has internalised and what sets of goals the person is trying, often unconsciously, to achieve. As internalised in a particular life, much of social structure is set in the realm of the unspoken norm that is most powerful when it dominates a person's life unawares.

Social structure is like the underground transportation system of a large city. The system is essential to the city's transportation needs but is for the most part invisible above ground. Even below ground, the passenger is aware of being on or in the system but still cannot see it as a system or get much sense of its complexity. One's main experience of the system is of the immediate vehicle one is in. For the unthinking that experience of a single vehicle and of bits and pieces of the system represents the whole system. Even this analogy, however, has its limits, for it places the person within the system, whereas social reality also has an unfailing way of putting the system within the person.

The task of those who would be faithful to young people, and even more so of those who would invite them to discipleship, is to help them break out of childhood naiveté about social structures and invite them to a lifetime journey to social awareness. To make even a beginning of this task is frustratingly slow. The most basic characteristic of the process is its gradualness. Progress here is as much marked by the asking of searching questions as by the giving of information. Compounding the frustration of slow progress is the arrival almost every year of a new 'generation' of the socially naive, with whom the process must begin all over again. In working with the young on these matters those who prefer styles of exuberant enthusiasm and immediate response are certain to be disappointed—one possible reason why Cardijn's approach of see-judge-act seems in many countries to have been replaced by more ebullient and 'effective' strategies.[21]

5. A FRUITFUL YOUTH PASTORATE

What then are the possibilities of undertaking this task with young people? Except for Cardijn, the person who has most helped youth workers both understand the fact of the submerged consciousness and see the possibilities of leading persons out of such a consciousness to a new position or perspective, has been Brazilian educator, Paulo Freire.[22] He has shown how problem-posing strategies can help persons question taken-for-granted social arrangements and come to view them from a position of fresh perspective. From the new position, social reality no longer seems to be some sort of divinely arranged, unquestionable entity. It appears instead as a series of human arrangements devised for the benefit of particular groups at particular times and to the disadvantage of other groups. Realising that social structures are human arrangements and thus open to question and revision gives a person a hermeneutical key with which to pry open any and every aspect of social reality.

According to Freire, what gives many persons access to the hermeneutical key with which to unlock the mysteries of social structures is a situation of oppression.

By being challenged over and over again to face and question the situation of injustice in which they find themselves, even illiterate persons can become knowledgeable and articulate about the causes and remedies of their oppression. In contrast, for young people in countries of the economic first world, their own comfortable situations in social structures fostering their own privileges and favouring their interests would seem to offer slight chance of moving them from an unquestioning stance to a consciousness ready to question and critique.

However, all young people in our day have available to them a hermeneutical key with which they can gain access to social reality from a position of acute questioning, and that key is the threat of nuclear holocaust. At the heart of modern life lurks an insanity that potentially questions every social structure. There is something dramatically wrong with a world ready to blow itself up and risk snuffing out forever the human experiment. Even quite young children have been known to express with simple insight the conviction, 'This is crazy. Why would anyone want to blow up the whole world?' In a world where every city has now become Hiroshima, more sophisticated young people can ask, 'How has this situation come to pass? What are we trying to protect that is worth risking all of life?'[23] It is as if smoke were billowing out of a tunnel of the underground transportation system and calling attention not only to the system hidden there but to the evident fact that something seriously wrong is happening there.

Would that it were not so, but the fact remains that life in the nuclear shadow offers immense possibilities to those interested in developing social awareness among youth. Of course these possibilities must be intelligently studied and pursued. For example, youth in the nations of economic privilege face the danger that their concern for human survival can become fixated at the level of concern for the survival, not so much of the race, but of their own privileges. While self-interest marks all persons, the self-interest of the middle and upper classes in consumerist cultures has about it an edge of narcissistic self-preoccupation.[24] The unspoken assumption that the survival of *our* class and of *our* nation is a special concern because *we* are superior—this assumption may have to be directly challenged.

6. NON-VIOLENCE, SOLIDARITY AND RESISTANCE

As one probes the questions raised by the nuclear arms race, ultimately one should come to issues of social justice. There is no adequate understanding of issues of peace without a clear understanding of their relationship to economic exploitation.[25] To deal with questions of deterrence, as did various national groups of bishops in their pastoral messages on peace in 1983,[26] as if these strategies affected only a 'balance of power' is to ignore the root economic underpinnings of the problem. In a world that has been on a war footing since 1938, with vast profits for those investing in military production, Western nations, in order to legitimate the continued military focus of their industrial system, would have had to invent the Soviet Union did it not exist.

Most of the above issues could be raised with youth by non-religious persons of good will, whose efforts would contribute to the human good. Followers of Jesus bring to their understanding additional 'keys' for interpreting their world. The key of non-violence, based on the words and example of Jesus appears to be particularly important in a world characterised by fundamental patterns of violence. Many young people know neither Jesus' teachings on this matter nor the tradition of non-violence found, however obscurely, in every period of the Christian era.[27] This teaching and tradition made accessible to youth could provide a valuable perspective from which to examine modern life. Never easily or glibly adopted, non-violence will offer young people who espouse it a radical, counter-cultural way of being in the world.

A similar radical perspective—and a related one—is that of solidarity with victims. Once accepted as a way of following the example of Jesus, solidarity with victims subverts the consumerist culture of violence.[28] It involves paying attention to the concrete effects of injustice and to the social evil causing such injustice. Whereas some strategies of what is mistakenly called evangelisation call young people to leap upon the Jesus-bandwagon (in the parade devoted to middle-class self-affirmation), solidarity with victims is a matter of gradual transformative growth in commitments that of their very nature caution against quick adoption. For most young people such slow growth will need the concrete example of others trying to live in such solidarity. The Jesus such persons follow will bear no resemblance to the sweet Jesus of sentimental religious art, but neither will he be as boring.

Life in the nuclear shadow inevitably forces us to re-examine accepted approaches to youth and to probe the implications for young people of the invitation to discipleship. Renewed youth ministry will be especially wary of fostering in young people the legitimation of political and social power that now holds all the world hostage to its greed. Unfortunately, not all adults working with youth in the economic first world have themselves thought through the implications of the nuclear threat for followers of Jesus. Those who have will find that the nuclear shadow is not the disease but a symptom that calls for a special kind of spirituality for young people today. The spirituality they must propose is a spirituality of resistance to all that is inhuman in life.

Religious work with youth in the past has put far more focus and stress on gaining the compliance of young people than on encouraging their resistance. The two of course are related. Knowing what things to resist is the other side of knowing the things to assist. If youth begins to resist militarism and its attendant violence; greed and its attendant self-preoccupation; and dominative patterns of thought and action, with their tendency to reduce other persons to objects, then possibly they can also assist solidarity across sexual, class, and national barriers.

There are obvious problems in the proposals made here. They raise many questions about the consciousness of adult Christians today and about the kind of Church that deserves the attention of youth. Also, solidarity with victims, the option of non-violence, and a spirituality of resistance will not appeal to all young people. Most likely, such a programme will be embraced only partially and gradually, but such is the way of growth, not only for youth but for disciples of all ages. The present state of youth ministry in the Church shows us that some leaders prefer a pied piper approach to youth, marching them along to the sound of a sweet tune. In the fairy tale of that name, however, the pied piper was basically one who betrayed the children who followed him.

Finally, the spirituality for youth facing the humanly created apocalypse is a spirituality of hope. Such a spirituality is worked out in the face of its opposite, despair.[29] To move to hope from despair is a much more complex, gradual, and dangerous task than to move to optimism from pessimism. There is no true Christian hope that has not looked evil in the eye, chosen to resist it with all one's might, and put the final overcoming in the hands of a loving God who does not give injustice the final say. Such was the adult hope that Jesus embodied. It is the only form of hope appropriate for young people living in the nuclear shadow.

Notes

1. Theodore Draper 'Nuclear Temptations' *NY Review of Books* (18 Jan 1984) 48.

2. '. . . moral courage has its source in . . . identification through one's sensitivity with the suffering of one's fellow human beings. I am tempted to call this "perceptual courage" because it depends on one's capacity to perceive, to let oneself see the suffering of other people. If we let ourselves experience the evil, we will be forced to do something about it.' Rollo May *The Courage to Create* (New York 1976), p. 8.

3. William Beardslee and John Mack 'The Impact on Children and Adolescents of Nuclear Developments' in Rita Rogers, *et al.*, *Psychosocial Aspects of Nuclear Developments* Task Force Report 20 (Washington, DC: American Psychiatric Assn., 1982), p. 91.

4. Sibylle Escalona 'Children and the Threat of Nuclear War' in *Behavioral Science and Human Survival* Milton Schwebel, (Palo Alto, California 1965) pp. 3–24.

5. *Ibid.* pp. 4–5.

6. *Ibid.* p. 5.

7. *Ibid.* p. 11.

8. *Ibid.* p. 15.

9. *Ibid.* p. 17.

10. Beardslee and Mack, p. 90.

11. Escalona, p. 19.

12. See Robert Jay Lifton 'Beyond Nuclear Numbing' *Teachers College Record* 84:1 (1982): 15–29, and 'The Psychic Toll of the Nuclear Age' NY *Times Magazine* (26 Sept 1982) 52ff.

13. Escalona, pp. 19–20.

14. Robert Coles 'Children and the Nuclear Bomb' forthcoming as a chapter of Robert Coles *The Moral Life of Children* (Boston 1985).

15. Coles' essay includes a useful review of this research literature, as does the essay of Beardslee and Mack, cited in note 3, pp. 64–73.

16. US Bureau of the Census, Current Population Reports, P-23, No. 114, *Characteristics of American Children and Youth, 1980* (Washington, DC: US Government Printing Office, 1982), p. 35. For an examination of the social as well as the psychic roots of a particular adolescent's suicide, see, John Mack and Holly Hickler *Vivienne: The Life and Suicide of an Adolescent Girl* (New York 1982).

17. Edward Wynne 'Adolescent Alienation and Youth Policy' *Teachers College Record* 78:1 (1976) 27.

18. 'Characteristics' p. 13.

19. Bayard Webster 'Health Chief Cites Rise in Violent Deaths of Young' NY *Times* (27 Oct 1982).

20. The notion of submerged consciousness is found in Paulo Freire 'Cultural Action and Conscientization' *Harvard Educational Review* 40: 3 (1970): 452–477. It has been reprinted as Chapter 7 of Paulo Freire, *The Politics of Education* (Massachusetts 1985) pp. 67–96.

21. Such strategy can be found in youth weekends that stress religious self-affirmation usually in an apolitical, class-stratified groups of young people. For a critique, see M. Warren 'New Stage in Weekend Retreats for Teens' *Origins* 14:6 (21 June 1984) 90–96. An important essay providing background toward a critique is Gregory Baum 'Theology Questions Psychiatry' *The Ecumenist* 20:4 (May–June 1982) 55–59.

22. See *Pedagogy of the Oppressed* (New York 1970) and *Education for Critical Consciousness* (New York 1973).

23. For an account of how statespersons, negotiators, and technicians alike have drifted away from these fundamental questions, see Thomas Powers 'What Is It About?' *The Atlantic Monthly* (Jan 1984) 35–55.

24. See Dorothee Soelle 'The Need for Liberation in a Consumerist Society' in *The Challenge of Liberation Theology*, eds., Mahan and Richesin (New York 1981) pp. 4–16.

25. See Bishop Roger Mahony 'Adverse Effects of the Arms Race in the Third World' *Origins* 14:4 (7 June 1984) 55–60.

26. About the same time in 1983, the episcopal conferences of the United States, France, Germany, Belgium, The Netherlands, and Japan issued pastoral statements on peace. These messages—with the exception of that of the Japanese bishops—tend to overlook the suffering caused in the Southern Hemisphere by the arms race of nations of the North. The East-West ideological polarity masks the underlying North-South polarity, which is economic and at root a question of justice rather than of creed. In comparing these pastoral statements, note how the Japanese bishops frame their thoughts with attention to the economic injustice of the arms race. Young people will need the economic critique in order to fully assess the ideological conflict. The texts of the pastorals of the US and French bishops are in *Origins*, 13 (1983); the texts of the others can all be found in *La Documentation Catholique* (1983), Nos. 1846 and 1863.

27. For a scholarly treatment, see Jean-Michel Hornus *It is Not Lawful for Me to Fight: Early Christian Attitudes Toward War, Violence and the State* (Scottsdale, Pennsylvania 1980).

28. Youth Workers would do well to study and draw out the implications for their ministry of the following work: Matthew L. Lamb *Solidarity with Victims: Toward a Theology of Social Transformation* (New York 1982).

29. A very important book about facing despair, though not written from a Christian persperctive is: Joanna Rogers Macy *Despair and Personal Power in the Nuclear Age* (Philadelphia 1983).

PART V

Alternative Responses to a Hopeful Future

Ans Joachim van der Bent

Youth in the World Council of Churches

THE STORY of youth in the World Council of Churches started in 1948 when the Council was founded at its First Assembly in Amsterdam. The story of youth in the ecumenical movement, however, had an earlier beginning. 'We turn to the young of all countries. With keen appreciation we have heard of their aspirations and efforts for a better social order as expressed in the youth movements of many lands. We desire to enlist the ardour and energy of youth, the freshness and fullness of their life, in the service of the Kingdom of God and of humanity.'[1] These sentences were part of the message of the First Universal Christian Conference on Life and Work which took place in Stockholm in 1925. The conference was the first large-scale attempt to get separated and isolated churches of many countries to collaborate on common tasks. The Continuation Committee of Life and Work appointed a Commission that was to ensure cooperation with young people.

'Youth to-day is really in an unenviable situation. It is conscious of the epic of the days of the Great War and realises that it lives in days of an aftermath. It wants something big to challenge it to be as great as the youth of two decades ago.'[2] So said J. C. Bacon when he introduced the World Alliance for Promoting International Friendship through the Churches and its concern for youth in a pamphlet in 1931. The World Alliance was founded at Constance, Germany, in 1914, and maintained a close relationship with the Church Peace Union through the years. A Youth Commission was appointed in 1932 and Dietrich Bonhoeffer became one of the three youth secretaries.

The constituencies as well as the objectives of the Universal Christian Council for Life and Work and the World Alliance for International Friendship through the Churches were at so many points the same, particularly in the realm of youth concerns, that a joint Ecumenical Youth

Commission was set up in 1933. Through collaboration with other international youth movements, such as the World Alliance of YMCAs, the World YWCA and the World Student Christian Federation, the Commission transmitted to young people's groups of the churches the essential values of the corresponding work of the world Christian youth movements. Its work grew steadily through the sponsoring of annual international and regional conferences for Christian youth leaders, the preparation of a group of young Christians to take part in the Second World Conference on Church and Society at Oxford in 1937, and the planning for the First World Conference of Christian Youth at Amsterdam in 1939.

'Christus Victor', the main theme of this very carefully prepared international youth gathering, was not only a motto, but became a truth, a vision and a reality for the participants. It broke down dividing walls of denomination, culture, history and race and strengthened the hidden bonds of a world-wide fellowship. The two great centres of discovery were the Bible studies and worship services. The facts of tragic division and isolation were most strongly felt in the different services of Holy Communion. The presence of many young Orthodox marked Amsterdam 1939. An international conference of Orthodox youth had already been held at Salonika, Greece, in 1930. No other ecumenical gathering has been so frequently celebrated and commemorated in subsequent years than the First World Conference of Christian Youth. A second world conference took place at Oslo in 1947; a third at Kottayam, India, in 1952. Regional youth conferences followed in Lausanne (1960), Ann Arbor (1962), Nairobi (1962–3), the Philippines (1964), and Broumana (1964).

1. THE YOUTH DEPARTMENT OF THE WCC

At the beginning of the Provisional Committee of the World Council of Churches at Geneva in 1946 the setting up of a Youth Department of the Council was approved which was directly to be attached to the General Secretariat. In 1954 it became a department within the Division of Ecumenical Action. It was commissioned to represent the World Council on the World Christian Youth Commission which included the World Alliance of YMCAs, the World YWCA, the World Christian Student Federation and the World Council of Christian Education and Sunday School Association. This body sponsored Oslo 1947 and several subsequent youth conferences.

The Youth Department of the World Council organised during several decades Annual European Youth Leaders Conferences which were mostly held near Geneva. In the early years much attention was given to the reconstruction of youth work in wartorn Europe. At later conferences national correspondents worked out the policy and programme for the region. The Youth Department cooperated with the Ecumenical Institute at Bossey in arranging courses for youth leaders. *Ecumenical Work Camps* became a wellknown and regular feature of the work of the Youth Department. Thousands of campers from many countries and confessions became aware of their responsibility to work for the unity and renewal of their churches, gained a clearer conception of the relevance of their faith to their daily life, and enabled them to be confronted with the socio-economic and political issues in their communities. Camps increased in variety and there was a significant expansion of ecumenical work camps in Africa, Asia and later Latin America.

Five kinds of activities were facilitated by *World Youth Projects*: leadership training, literature for youth work, visits of leaders between countries or continents, the establishing of youth centres, and the provision of full time interdenominational youth workers. *Youth Voluntary Service* was a programme resulting from numerous requests received from young people who desired to give a short period of voluntary, unskilled service whenever there was need. Many international consultations were organised by the Youth Department in the fifties and sixties on specific themes and concerns, such as the Place and Function of Youth Work in the Church, Baptism and Confirmation, Holy Communion and Youth, the Missionary Structure of the Congregation, Confessionalism and the Ecumenical Movement, Youth in a Complex Society, Conversion in a Secular Age. The Youth Department produced numerous books, pamphlets, reports and serial publications which were widely distributed to churches and youth organisations in all continents.

The Second Assembly at Evanston in 1954 was reminded of the fact that many young people leave the Church at an age when they might be expected to come into responsible membership of it. During the following years a thorough study on 'The Integration of Youth in the Life and Mission of the Church' was undertaken. In many encounters and discussions older and younger Christians were forced to rethink the evangelistic task of youth itself, and the nature of the preparation for full Church membership carried out by the churches and of the commitment manifested by young people.

Both a World Teaching Conference at Strasbourg, in July 1960, organised by the World Student Christian Federation, and the almost simultaneously held Ecumenical Youth Assembly at Lausanne, sponsored by the World Council of Churches, revealed that youth rejected the notion of integration. In spite of the eloquent addresses of well-known theologians and Church leaders, the audience was restless. There was too much speaking about the life of the Church; what youth wanted was action in the world. Instead of mission in traditional terms youth emphasised involvement in modern society.

Disillusionment was expressed not only with the structures of the churches, but with the institutional framework of the ecumenical movement. There was a deep sense of disappointment that after several decades of living together the churches had not solved the distressing problem of intercommunion. What really kept young Christians apart? It was the Taizé community that started to recognise the spiritual needs of the young generation. 'Intercommunion is not a question between denominations but between nations; not of intercommunion between all sorts of confessions but between all sorts of people. Communion is the first fulfillment of the "feast that the Lord will make for all nations, according to Isaiah 25:6" ' (Johannes Hoekendijk).[3]

In spite of ecumenical attempts during the sixties to shift the concern for the integration of youth into the life of the Church to a concern for the contribution young Christians can make to the missionary outreach of the Church, the interest of youth in churchly ecumenism increasingly faded. It lost confidence in conferences and study programmes as it saw little sense in the investment of more time in the creation of ecumenical ideas and plans if the cheques the previous generation had signed were not cashed first. Christian education was no more seen as a preparation for life, but as a commentary on it, written from the perspective of involvement. The voice of authority, whether it criticised or endorsed young people's actions, was only heard and accepted when it spoke from within the struggle for an authentic Christian presence in the world.

2. YOUTH IN GOD'S WORLD

Youth in God's World remains undoubtedly one of the most searching and advanced documents which the Youth Department of the World Council of Churches has ever produced. It was included in the Work Book for the Fourth Assembly at Uppsala in 1968. The document honestly admitted that 'youth can experiment courageously and dangerously with traditions and reject inherited value systems. The search for security can make them also ruthlessly egocentric and conservative.' It is not youth which is the hope of the future, but the future which is the hope of youth. Translating the destructive conflict between generations into a productive tension is difficult. Education of adults is as much needed as education for young people. But more than education is necessary. 'Only when young and old will accept the challenge of a common future together and build their lives into service, will the conflict disappear and the tension become productive . . . Separate youth work, which does not aim at a reconciliation of the generations and does not make this aim visible in its activities, does not belong to the Church.'

The last sentence should not be interpreted in a churchly context. The paper made it clear that youth work should be mainly organised secularly. The churches should offer services to young people—space to meet, chance to be together with the older generation—'whether this brings to, or keeps young people in the Church or not'. The document also issued a strong warning against the idolising of youth, because many young people know very well that they are not better off or worse than older people. The romantic evaluation of their contributions to Church and society sounds to them like a new form of paternalism. Enthusiastic applause for protest is as harmful as authoritarian refusal to identify its causes. Protest in itself is not enough; it has to be evaluated, deepened and translated in a constructive contribution. It is not sentimentality, therefore, that is sought, nor a demonstration of understanding, but genuine confidence that a new generation can and will contribute to the welfare of the community. Such confidence must be shown in an invitation to partnership. This implies that the greatest mistake would be to demand that young people solve their personal problems independently of the great problems of our time.

In its conclusion *Youth in God's World* stated: '. . . A youth ministry should . . . never become a nervous effort to keep young people in or win them for the Church. A style of life which is inspired by the Gospel and a genuine care for a new generation is all that is required. The message of good news is strong enough to excite, engage and commit those of all ages.'[4]

The political enthusiasm, the ecumenical iconoclasm and the quest for radical Christian ethics of youth reached their climax at the Uppsala Assembly. In the whole history of the ecumenical movement youth had never been so visibly present and outspoken in criticism of adult deliberations. Common means of expression in the form of sit-in, stand-up, walk-out, picketing, sit-down, boycott were used. Youth produced its own newspaper *Hot News*. It raised a storm of protest that the average age of the voting delegates was over fifty while young people had no voting power at all. There was a strong conviction that disunity among Christians is caused by basic human conflicts. The churches should render a common service to the poor, the suffering and the exploited of the world and so demonstrate that they maintain the same apostolic faith, proclaim the same Gospel, break the same bread, and unite in common prayer.

After 1969 the staff of the WCC Youth Department was considerably reduced and lost financial allocations. Under a new integration policy youth concerns and programmes were to be dealt with throughout the World Council, from 1971 onwards particularly in Programme Unit III on Education and Renewal. 'Yet, in effect,' according to the *Uppsala to Nairobi* report, 'youth as a constituency was obscured and seemed to become the object of benign neglect.'⁵ Youth indeed was hardly visible at the Fifth Assembly in Nairobi in 1975. During the seventies the sub-unit on Youth organised considerably fewer consultations and conferences than in previous periods as ecumenical youth work became increasingly a hazardous affair. On the whole the younger generation in the North Atlantic was unclear in its direction yet searching for meaning and purpose; its counterpart in the Southern hemisphere was partly struggling for justice, both within and outside of the churches and the ecumenical movement. There was a dialectical tension between the two developments.

3. BETWEEN NAIROBI AND VANCOUVER

Not surprisingly one of the primary aims of the sub-unit on Youth in the period between Nairobi 1975 and Vancouver 1983 has been 'to achieve adequate representation of young people on the staff, commissions, programmes and decision-making bodies of the WCC, as well as in the ecumenical movement as a whole'. It concentrated in particular on the stewards' programme making the service of young people available to major international conferences and the annual meetings of the Central Committee. But the sub-unit admitted that 'it must find ways to enable youth in greater numbers to contribute their insights to the ecumenical movement'.⁶

After this short survey of the involvement of youth in the ecumenical movement and in the World Council of Churches, one of the major instruments of that movement, it is appropriate to call the attention to the wisdom of four church leaders and theologians: Dietrich Bonhoeffer, who was much involved in ecumenical youth work in the thirties; Albert H. van den Heuvel, Executive Secretary of the Youth Department from 1964–8; Philip A. Potter, Executive Secretary of the Youth Department from 1957–60 and General Secretary of the World Council from 1972–84; and W. A. Visser 't Hooft, the Council's first General Secretary until 1966.

In 1934 Bonhoeffer wrote a number of theses on youth work. Young people, according to him, have no special status or privilege within the Christian community. 'They should serve the community by listening to the Gospel, by learning and practising it.'⁷ Only the Church counts; Christian youth organs are but makeshifts and have only relative importance. Albert H. van den Heuvel came in 1965 to the conclusion 'that youth work is allowed only because of the hardness of our hearts; it must be seen under the aspect of God's patience rather than God's will. Youth work in the Church is an anomaly, like denominations and rummage sales. They may be allowed, but they are not self-evident . . . Where the *ekklesia* is discovered, the generations are united.'[8]

Philip Potter addressed many ecumenical gatherings on the question of service to youth. At the Third Assembly in New Delhi in 1961 he said: 'We are in serious danger of driving young people to despair of the churches and therefore in flight from them' and the work of the Church 'may perish for lack of younger men and women to take it up, because they despair of anything really happening in it'. Concerning the intricate problem of intercommunion, for youth especially a matter of confusion and dismay, Philip Potter exclaimed: 'Intercommunion is not a battle-cry of Protestant malcontents shrilly outcried by well-armed Catholic stalwarts. It is the deepest inner reality of the People of God without which they cannot truly render a common witness to the world.'[9]

Deeply concerned about the future of youth from his early ecumenical career onwards, W. A. Visser 't Hooft predicted in 1959 that the student conference in Strasbourg the next year would deal with fundamental issues and spoke of giving 'young people that "mountain-top vision" (as John R. Mott used to call it) of the comprehensive calling of the Church and its mission in and to the world, which is the ABC of a dynamic ecumenical movement'.[10] Confronted with the slowness of their elders and their churches, he called young people at the New Delhi assembly 'to work, pray and sweat' for the cause of Christian unity at all levels.

The first two statements seem to contradict the last two statements, but in fact they are complementary. Since the beginning of service to youth in the ecumenical movement to the present day one can speak of a process of development or a cycle of evolution. God's history with his people means ever new human possibilities. Generations are the bearers of the new in his creative work. In youth we can discern God's continuity of life, its rhythm of preparation and accomplishment. The history of youth in the World Council of Churches is a story of stages of one single and visible community of two generations, the call to the integration of youth in the life of the established Church, the participation of youth in the mission and service of the Church, the conflict of and the separation between the older and younger generations, the necessity for Christian youth to testify to God's freedom and to *be* the Church *now* in their sector of the world's life.

Although the sixties were the most exciting, creative and controversial period, all stages were marked by trial and error, advancement and stagnation, whether youth was in agreement, or in conflict with—or indifferent—to the Church. It cannot be otherwise because youth is always exposed to crises and challenges in the Church and in the world. Its search for unity and reconciliation has met with success during certain periods; it failed at other times.

4. ENCOUNTER BETWEEN GENERATIONS

These facts today clearly reveal that there is a dialectical process of dynamic encounter between generations. Adult attitudes of distrust, abandonment, admiration and nostalgia are in a sense adolescent and misplaced. The old generation should have learned by not to be on its guard that its old ways of life and its old words of wisdom are not causing unnecessary, even tragic, antagonism. At some moments of history not adolescence but adulthood has to go. On the other hand, questioning the spiritual and ethical realms of the old generation, young men and women can overshoot the mark and become self-contained and self-defeating. At some moments of history not adulthood but adolescence has to go.

Successes in the earlier period should not be underestimated. Addressing the Pre-Assembly Youth Event of the Vancouver Assembly of the World Council of Churches in July 1983, Philip Potter reminded the participants of various contributions which the youth made to the ecumenical movement. After the war young people were immediately engaged in acts of reconciliation through ecumenical work camps in Europe and Asia. They 'were deeply involved in issues of the renewal of the Church—the Church being the "laos", the laity, the whole people of God'. Young people first shared the idea of ecumenical sharing of resources by starting World Youth Projects.

'It was through the Youth Department that the Orthodox were invited to meet together to form SYNDESMOS', the World Federation of Orthodox Youth Organisations. 'That is one contribution. The other contribution came after the Third Assembly: it was youth who brought Roman Catholics as youth consultants to assemblies.' Youth has been 'in the forefront of the issues of justice; for example, urban and industrial mission and urban-rural mission have been largely young people's involvement'. Lastly, 'a further contribution of youth has been to promote regional ecumenism. Even before the formation of regional councils of churches, there existed ecumenical youth organisations. Latin America and Europe are examples of this.'[11]

But neither should the failures from the early seventies onwards be underestimated. The counter-cultures and new religions of youth were not critically analysed and evaluated from sociological, economic and psychological perspectives. The churches neglected to examine the cultural and ideological dimensions of their own existence, particularly in relation to the predicament and the behaviour of the young generation. The fact that this number of *Concilium* deals extensively with the question of the future of youth testifies to the urgency of interdisciplinary, systematic and comprehensive inquiry into alternatives of meaning and search for purposefulness for humanity moving towards the year 2000.

God's new creation is not being fashioned in a vacuum since it is the redemption of the created world—the contemporary world conditioned by a revolution in sexuality, the deep impact of prolonged scientific education, the lure of consumption and leisure, the inclination toward ideological conformity or counter-cultural permissiveness, the disturbance of personality caused by unfinished mental and emotional growth, the disintegration of family ties and tribal bonds, the unpredictable and manipulated labour market for youth, the challenges of political commitment to matters of peace, justice and the integrity of creation or the cultivation of visibly limited but meaningful human relations.

Precisely in all these crises and opportunities it is not unlikely that the ministry of Christian youth is at the threshold of unexpected new ways of concerted action and exploration. Our clear-sightedness and keen sense of hearing are newly tested. *New* ecumenical structures of communication, learning and sharing need to be devised in order that youth makes again *its* contribution to a *new* ecumenical adventure. As youth has become more versatile and circumspect today than during the period around the year 1968, it needs to be encouraged to express itself more explicitly on issues of power, culture, dialogue and spirituality which preoccupy the World Council of Churches at present.

Even more than the old generation young people are deeply aware of and oppose the increasing intransigence, irrationality and inhumanness of concentrated political, economic, technological and military power which undergirds the doctrine of national security. They also expose and resist the mysterious powers of ecclesiastical institutions, so far only partly demythologised. Christian youth searches and yearns for a power which absorbs 'powerful power' rather than counters power with power.

5. YOUTH AND A WORLD CHURCH

Youth lives in the plural wonder of cultures and realises that listening to and receiving from receptor cultures is an essential part of witnessing to God's salvation of the world. It joyfully acknowledges that Christ both judges and transcends Western confessionalism and denominationalism in their cultural settings. Youth has begun to glimpse the possibilities and the implications of cultural diversity taken absolutely seriously in the context of the ecumenical activity of God. The creative indigenous resources for understanding the Gospel afresh are not to be found in any one centre, but throughout the whole world.

In the realm of dialogue with people of other living faiths, youth is less burdened and conditioned than the old generation to experience in various ways that dialogue is a progressive and cumulative process, which does not only take place through verbal communication, but through the dynamic contact of life with life. Genuine dialogue is essential to dispel condescending attitudes Christians have towards people of other faiths, which makes proclamation ineffective and irrelevant. Youth needs to be stimulated and can teach the old generation that both a risk as well as a deep sense of vocation are required to enter into dialogue with an open mind and heart to others.

The search for and the sharing of a new spirituality is undoubtedly vital for the life of Christian congregations. But it is still more important to raise the consciousness of the people of God at the grass roots as to why and how their way of spirituality and mode of worship are influenced by a religiously conditioned culture. Youth is not afraid to share in different spiritualities without lapsing into a dangerous syncretism. African and Asian spiritualities can be channels of deep adoration and humility.

The overall theme 'The Unity of the Church and the Renewal of Human Community' has been on the Council's agenda for fifteen years, but little progress has been made so far in relating the two dynamically to each other. Youth could demonstrate on its own new ways of faith and life that both the potential unity of the world, in the midst of its division and brokenness, and the urgent renewal of the Church are the goal of God's universal salvation. It needs new youthful insight and courage to stress that the Church is but a function of human community until the kingdom arrives.

As the household of God, of which youth is always an integral part, the Church can only be a sign of promise to an evolving society it it is first of all a true sign of God's judgment and reconciliation. The being of this sign is more a matter of a clumsy posture, stammering speech and concealed expectation than eloquent and lofty public affirmation. It corresponds with the ardour and freshness of youth as it continues to struggle for an authentic presence in the world.

Notes

1. The Stockholm Conference. The Official Report of the Universal Christian Conference on Life and Work, ed. G. K. A. Bell (London 1926) p. 714.
2. J. C. Bacon *Recruiting for Peace. The World Alliance and Youth* (London 1931) p. 3.

3. Johannes Hoekendijk 'Exceptions, Eschatology and Our Common Practices' *Youth* (Dec. 1962) 75.

4. Work Book for the Assembly Committees (Uppsala, Sweden 4–19 July 1968) (Geneva: WCC, 1968) pp. 138, 141, 149, 152.

5. Uppsala to Nairobi, 1968–1975 ed. David E. Johnson. (New York, London 1975) p. 202.

6. Nairobi to Vancouver, 1975–1983. (Geneva: WCC, 1983) pp. 209 and 213.

7. Dietrich Bonhoeffer *Gesammelte Schriften*. 3 (Munich 1960) p. 292.

8. Albert H. van den Heuvel 'A Short and Critical History of Youth' *The New Creation and the New Generation* (New York 1965) pp. 75 and 79.

9. Philip A. Potter 'Going Forward Together Into Manifest Unity *Ecumenical Review*, 14, No. 3, (April 1962), 345 and 347.

10. Minutes and Reports of the Twelfth Meeting of the Central Committee of the World Council of Churches, Rhodes, Greece, 19–27 August 1959 (Geneva 1959) p. 99.

11. Philip A. Potter 'Youth and the Ecumenical Movement' *Youth Newsletter*, 7, No. 3, (Sept. 1983) p. 5.

Jacques Grand'Maison

The Challenge of Youth:
A New Prophetic Paradigm

I WISH to show how the challenge posed by young people at this turning-point of history can give rise to a new prophetic paradigm which is both theological and politological. This paradigm features an astonishing dialectical conjunction: that of a far-reaching renewal of the complex of social problems and an unprecedented pursuit of conversion, and even a theological reinterpretation of the Message itself. This synthetic process depends on four inseparable co-ordinates: *faith in the future* as against a logic of dissolution which threatens the present-day world; the revolt of the individual and collective *subject*; the involvement of a *third force* in history as in trinitarian eschatology; and liberation of the *Other* and by the Other. My article is intended to supply not only a framework to aid understanding but a social, pastoral and theological praxis.

1. FAITH IN THE FUTURE IN THE FACE OF A DEATH-LOGIC

It may seem rather paradoxical to discuss youth without a future when the two concepts are connected almost by nature. Young people (and this point is made more than once in this *Concilium*) embody the future of all societies and link that future, which is also the future of all mankind, to our present moment. They provide not only the most vital of human dreams and aspirations, but a yardstick for the truth of the most decisive attitudes and forms of behaviour.

Christians are especially affected by a challenge of this kind, and on several counts. That is not surprising, for they enact the prophetic awareness and praxis of a God who 'outflanks history' and brings the covenant of the Kingdom and the future of mankind together in Jesus Christ. There we have a new heaven and a new earth: 'already' but 'not yet'. This historical and eschatological discrepancy is a paschal drama, and young people desperately anxious about the future may be the privileged agents of its disclosure. In so doing they not only underline the most heinous sins of an age but stress its due graces of deliverance and salvation.

These are not abstract considerations. Let us look at the realities and actual signs, the relevance and prophetic 'bite' of which are etched in the living flesh of our epoch.

The large-scale unemployment among young people is not merely an economic tragedy and a political and material responsibility, but a spiritual problem which is hardly ever faced up to. In fact, this crucial problem serves to reveal our deepest attitudes, our most authentic and decisive thoughts about the future. In this area more than any other, perhaps, we have to consider long-term investments and sacrifices which are so considerable that they demand spiritual strength, moral excellence, a source of firm motivation, and a qualitatively extraordinary faith, love and hope. Even though we should not ask God to supply what is lacking, and have to show the quality of our own courage, we are still assured of his saving power at this serious turning-point.

Faith in the future exists at the junction of our historical responsibility and Christ's own grace. Let us try to see more clearly the nature of this complex interplay of factors: a kind of *kairos* in the contemporary drama evident in the challenge of youth.

To bear a child today is more than a natural or rational endeavour; it is an act of faith. Here we have a pristine situation to point up the inadequacy of some dichotomies which degrade man and insult God. One of them is the false dichotomy of the so-called 'natural order' of creation versus the supernatural order of redemption which alone can summon the response of faith. There is also the false dichotomy of atheism—faith in man, and monotheism—faith in God. As the twentieth century draws to a close, everything amounts to an act of faith, especially in respect of the future. The Promethean myth of the Enlightenment, with its vision of unending progress, seems to have issued in the historical despair and absurdity of ephemeral man. The new atheism speaks of this 'insupportable triviality of being'. How then is it possible to establish policies or take risks to make the future viable for young people, if even faith in humankind is as unsure as that?

Christians have nothing to rejoice about in this confusion experienced by non-believers (in the sense of being without faith in God). Too many spiritualities of the Kingdom are based on a disavowal of the values of earthly life, historical responsibility and even mankind. Such spiritualities find it difficult to give an answer to the death logic which is especially strong in the Western world with all its problems of a falling birth-rate, nuclear threat, and recourse to a short-term philosophy in every area. Have we, and we Christians especially, tended to forget the faith of God in mankind which we find in Genesis. 'And God saw that it was good.' It is the creation which is original, and not sin, which is the seed of death. God has never gone back on his first commitment; he has never retracted the confidence which he placed in the full historical responsibility of human beings and their future. The promise was re-affirmed after the tragedy of the Flood: 'Seedtime and harvest will never cease'. Human beings made in the divine image express themselves and build the world in a living praxis whose foundation-stone is the resurrection of that Jesus who became Christ our Lord. To be sure, this fundamental praxis is unfolded in a process in which the temptation no longer to believe in mankind and that to cease believing in God are inseparable.

If we compare the gospels and Genesis we can move ahead from this point. The scandal of the Incarnation is not so much the divinity of Jesus as the incredible humanity of God in Jesus. The fact that God becomes the son of man in Jesus so that we may become children of God, qualifies not only the wonderful scandal of this good news, but a dramatic process which is hardly ever acknowledged: namely, that it is more difficult to believe in humankind than to believe in God, above all humankind in accordance with the God of Jesus: human beings are the bearers of the world's future in the process of the Kingdom. Therefore our faith in God is manifested by way of our faith in mankind, in the human future in history which is drawn ahead by a free Kingdom extending beyond our earthly horizons. What is in question, therefore, is *a single movement of faith* passing through history and kingdom, creation and salvation, flesh and spirit. Hence my rejection of the false dichotomies I mentioned earlier: dichotomies of the natural as against the supernatural order.

Confirming our faith in the future, and trying to shape it with and for young people, means locating ourselves in this fundamental praxis which is bound up with being a 'believer' and 'living' person oriented to an open future yet to be accomplished; a future founded in a Hope which works through and beyond this historical risk where the Promise of God and the Kingdom of the dead and risen Jesus reside. The God of the prophets and of Jesus might indeed have reason to move over to the side of those who have maintained a living praxis, and to leave a West which, however Christian in origin, could so easily capitulate to a logic of dissolution, even to the extent of taking chances with the future of its own children. 'After us the Flood' would seem to be the motto of my generation, the generation of prosperity which is nevertheless unable to hear the cries of a new generation which suddenly finds its way blocked, even when we have made it so many promises.

Should we need convincing otherwise, do I need to stress the extraordinary range of the action of a God who, in Jesus, declared his presence in the world under the characteristics and human status of a child? Did he wish to tell us that the crux of the meeting between him and us is to be found precisely in the fate of children, in the responsibility of those whom we have procreated, in the future which we accord them, and in the room for receptivity and initiative which we grant them? Why are we reluctant to think of young people as 'sacraments' of God the Father, of Jesus the Brother, and the Mother Spirit? And to think of them as 'sacraments' of the future in the Kingdom which brings together all scattered sons and daughters.

I have stressed this first component of the prophetic paradigm because it lies at the base of the three others which follow.

2. THE REVOLT OF THE INDIVIDUAL AND COLLECTIVE SUBJECT

Rubbing two stones together to produce fire, heat and light is like bringing the action of God in making himself a child in Jesus up against a major characteristic of present-day humankind: namely, the fact that the planet is largely inhabited by young people. They do not possess any automatic lease on power, property and knowledge. All they have to put in the scales is their human condition. We love a child for his or her own sake and not for any other reason. Otherwise we do not truly love the child. The same is true of God and us. Is it necessary to recall a particular theology of divine glory? God began by loving us for our own sakes, by treating us as free, responsible subjects, of value in our own right. It is in that way that we become capable (*capax Dei*) of loving God for his own sake, and not as an *object* of worship, an *instrument* of salvation. There are 'idolatrous' theologies, in the biblical sense. God-thing-object; man-thing of God. I say 'biblical' advisedly, because my theme goes beyond a mere metaphysical transition from object to subject. The reference to idolatry has much deeper connotations, above all when we think of the highly serious 'sin' which the Bible holds it to be.

Here too I must dot the 'i's in regard to contemporary history. Surely it is the young people who are *used* on a vast scale in wars of all kinds . . . Young people, essentially, are cannon-fodder. Through young people, as we have seen so often, nations have remained instruments and objects, and this is just as true of revolutions which were idealistic to begin with, but soon became mere transfers of power and property in which the people were not recognised as the authentic subject of history in everyday life as in politics. Many young people today are in a position to bear witness to a new post-capitalist and post-Marxist consciousness which might be summarised thus: almost everywhere in the world individuals, classes and nations rise up and ask: 'Are we of value for our own sakes, or are we no more than mere cogs in the machinery of your capital, technology or Party; in short, instruments of your history and not subjects of our own history?' This new awareness is to be found in many young groups. I shall return to this point, which is important in many ways.

We must not lose sight of our historical analysis, which shows that the revolution of the individual and collective subject has not yet occurred; that it is germinating in the very relationship which God set up between himself and us; and that it is at the heart of Jesus' evangelical practice. Whether it is a question of the Beatitudes or of the last Judgment, it is the poor—those who possess no more than their human condition—who are at the mid-point of the historical conjunction and the Kingdom. Young people, because of their powerlessness and lack of property, are able to profit from this purpose of God in Jesus. The Beatitudes ask us to share ourselves more than possessions. Above all, surely, we are asked to experience this basic process in the relation between generations? It is an experience of parents and children, of brothers and sisters. It is too glib to assert that a society cannot be organised on a family model. We might reply that without this fundamental human aspect, societies remain impervious to the demands of young people. I shall try to express this notion of the rebellion of the subject in less 'domestic' terms.

The basic human rights which are to some extent the new ethico-political ideal of contemporary humanity are highly contradictory in a way often common to 'right' and 'left'. Here we have societies which claim to be established on a basis of law and rights, in which those who have only their rights but no power to back them up have no weight whatsoever. What meaning does law or justice have in such a situation? The contradiction is glaring, and shows clearly that the revolution of the individual and collective subject has not yet been accomplished. I do not separate 'individual' from 'collective' because a virtually disenfranchised young person or pauper no longer has any freedom except in his or her own environment or class. We learn not to separate the dimensions of life among the 'little people', and to treat human beings as a whole, as 'subjects' therefore.

Some pertinent instance of this basic orientation is often to be found in the consciousness of the young. During a hearing of a case before a juvenile court in my country, a judge had just lectured a young person who had committed an offence and acknowledged his responsibility. Quite rightly, the judge reminded him of respect for the law and for the rights of others. The judge's legal and moral logic was faultless, and showed that everything had been heard, weighed, evaluated and judged. Before leaving the dock, the young person asked to speak. His speech was very short but very true in the circumstances: 'Your honour, I am more than what I have done'. This goes to show that a lively awareness of the 'subject' is no abstract thing in young persons. It also shows that even the most aware section of the adult world forgets it along the way. Perhaps that statement might be said to reflect the voice of God himself.

3. THE INVOLVEMENT OF THIRD PARTIES IN HISTORY AND TRINITARIAN ESCHATOLOGY

It is 'third parties' who manifest a consciousness and praxis of the individual and collective subject. Here too, we shall find evidence of the astonishing conjunction of a new complex of social problems and a trinitarian revelation.

The two major systems which dominate the world have a dualist logic as a common feature. On the one hand, there is capitalism established on the basis of a liberal contract and, on the other hand, Communism built upon a struggle between two basic classes. Neither in its historical praxis leaves room for a third force, for those without any weight or value in this game for two: either because such third parties have no possessions (in the liberal contract), or because they have no power (in the struggle between two classes). This dualism extends to many institutions subject to a pure relationship of force and with conflicting claims to sole and total power. In hospital or school strikes, for example, patients and children are not intimately concerned with the matter of the strike, yet they are the very reason why these institutions with an eminently humane purpose exist at all. Even worse, there are families in which the fights between adults are borne by the children who suffer them. That is the extent to which the savage reality of this kind of dualism can reach. The third parties are the children, those excluded from relations of power, and the Third World.

But it is children who exhibit the deepest aspects of this kind of process. As Truffaut shows in a famous film, *Pocket Money*, the child, unlike an adult, has no choice of an alternative course of action. Modern laws, for example, provide for various possible arrangements in the case of a divorce. How often a child finds himself or herself in a more or less excluded situation, on the edge, powerless. One is only five, or ten, or fifteen years old once in one's life. Childhood and adolescence are fragile states, and cannot be compared with adulthood, which can more easily adapt to alternative solutions. To be deprived of a father or mother, or of a caring household, cannot be equated with adults changing partners.

In poor environments, the effects are even more tragic since there are no resources to provide for two households, one for each of the separated parents, nor to pay for substitute solutions, such as a nanny, as the rich do. Yet again, we can see how the fate of young people is the yardstick for the humanity of a society, its social practices, and its cultural, economic and political tendencies. The child is a prototypical third party in respect of the dualist logic which has gradually established itself in the world, from the top (the two forms of imperialism) to the everyday basis where the young people pay the ghastly bill for adult battles.

The fate of third parties is the supreme yardstick of humanity. It is also the yardstick of evangelical practice, right up to the trinitarian economy. In St John, Jesus affirms that the decisive procedure is to be found in the coming of the third party: the Holy Spirit. 'And when he comes, he will convince the world concerning sin and righteousness and judgment . . . When the Spirit of truth comes, he will guide you into all the truth . . . [like a woman] in travail, she has sorrow because her hour has come; but when she is delivered of the child, she no longer remembers the anguish, for joy that a child is born into the world' (John 16:8, 13, 21).

This likeness of Spirit to child with their status as 'third parties' is most striking, for the 'third party' is the supreme communicator of the world's sin and the grace of salvation, and the one who uncovers 'justice and judgment', the 'whole truth' about history and the Kingdom. We are a long way from a chemically pure spiritual theology of the Holy Spirit. The Holy Spirit, through the third-party child, extends the historical economy of the Incarnation and the action of God himself, which passes through the excluded prophets and through Jesus, the One excluded from the power relations of his own time and ours. In this perspective, we see that the vision of the world and the historical praxis of Christianity is not binary but ternary, both on the human level and on God's level, in both socio-political and theological arenas. The Spirit who extends to all that lives is not the Spirit of sentimental spirituality but the 'salt of the earth' who restores the action of justice, and the longing to love, struggle, create and save. This salt is to be found above all in the living flesh of all the third parties of the earth, in the majority of its inhabitants—who are young people.

4. LIBERATION OF THE OTHER, BY THE OTHER

The tragic fate of young people in the Third World and in ours extends to the very depths of the present historical crisis, and calls for a radical conversion in which the most material may not be divorced from the most spiritual tasks. For us Christians, our daily bread and the eucharistic bread are both material and spiritual; all the more reason, then, for the same to be true of the child of our flesh and of our soul. What do we have to offer the rising generation? The latest motor car in the West, and in the Third World a war which serves as a battlefield for the two great forms of imperialism. There has been talk of a rising generation which has been sacrificed, and of a generation without purpose. Seen from the viewpoint of young people, the whole planet appears in the perspective of one and the same challenge: that of a savagery with a number of masks. In the rich countries, the prosperous generation holds on to its comfortable acquisitions even to the point of no longer wanting children, without taking into account its refusal to make the sacrifices which would be required by investments to overcome unemployment among young people. Through the indirect medium of that unemployment the rich countries will (perhaps?) be better able to understand not only the tragedy of the Third World but the need for a new economic order. The middle classes of the developed societies have been able to present a generous front by accepting social policies on education and health. But the policies they have adopted in this regard are not such as to disturb their socio-economic mobility.

The recent crisis puts the middle classes in a quite different context of solidarity. It is a solidarity with the poorest of all, which is much more expensive. The 'trend to the right' in so many rich countries is another indication of their pseudo-generosity in matters of social justice. The true sins of the developed societies are more clearly evident on their own ground, when they come face-to-face with their own poor and their own young people.

Let us see how young people can have a prophetic and political impact. First in respect of evangelical conversion. For Jesus, this not only reveals the true hidden sin, but the liberating issue. Let us see how young people lead us there. Psychology tells us that with the onset of maturity we begin to relativise money, work and social status, whereas for the adult his or her own children and their future become increasingly important. Here is the positive and liberating ferment which could be the human spur to that conversion of a prosperous generation which is so tempted to fall back 'collectively' on its acquisitions and say: 'After us the Flood!'

But the prophetic impact of young people is not restricted to this measure. Some new tendencies among young people have other goals, such as the search for an alternative society, or a desire to see things *differently*, to live in another way. For instance, it is probably the first time in human history that war has been called in question so radically. Surely it is a sign of the times that pacifist movements are recruiting so many members from among young people? In this area, as in so many others, young people become the *other*. This characterisation of the other emerges from conventional logic. It is a logic powerless to discover new solutions during crises the peculiarity of which is to disclose the dead-end to which the well-worn paths of a society which cannot renew itself all lead.

There is a well-known biblical event. After captivity in Egypt, the desert crisis provides the turning-point. The Lord of the Earth promises: the Other, who cannot be reduced to the level of any social system which is enclosed in an internal logic of homogenisation and is incapable of seeing things differently. Surely a legitimate prophetic practice is to see how the Other who is God does as is like the new and different aspects of the contributions made by the rising generation. Like Jesus, whom no one could suborn, the rising generation is in an evangelical situation: that is, they stand for non-violence and an imperative of social justice which is accompanied by inevitable conflicts. We must remember that the non-violent Jesus was fierce when faced with the dealers in the Temple. But the Jerusalem Temple was more than a religious location. It was the centre of power of the Jewish leaders and also a major location of socio-economic activity (we have only to think of animal sacrifices). Jesus' gesture in the Temple hit at the heart of the city. Hence the rejection of that Other who did not play the conventional game of logic and praxis. The struggle of the Cross had started decisively.

The fate of young people carries a similar evangelical discomfort with it: a message of brotherhood and peace which on its way meets the cross of injustice, which is also the cross of theology of power and death. Already, in the morning-time of the world, in Genesis, in spite of all the violence, the fundamental opposition, now more than ever before, is revealed in its absolutely naked truth: *brotherhood or death*. Surely that is the crucial choice for present-day humanity? The 'majority' comprised by the children of the planet make this plea now, when for the first time the men of war are able to destroy the earth totally. Until now, even though the hope was illusory, wars were an ultimate means of resolving conflicts and even of re-establishing economy and history. The chain of violence which René Girard puts at the centre of the entire human historical adventure—the violence with its mechanisms of scapegoat, combat between two parties, and absolute power— has reached its critical limit. It is absolutely necessary to leave this vicious circle and engage in a new praxis with the new things which can only come from the Other who is God in the risen Jesus. The drama of young people reveals prophetically the most heinous hidden sins of our age as it develops a deep crisis of hope, but the same young people are also the liberating and creating ferment actually incarnating the saving grace of a Kingdom, a new heaven and a new earth. I should like to express this major transition by closing with a minor event of the kind found in the gospels. It is the testimony of a young prisoner who was rehabilitated. 'I had begun to think that society, life, my life in fact, were just one big dung-heap. But when I read the gospel, I changed my way of thinking absolutely. After all, growers use dung to produce first-class vegetables and superb fruit. So I decided to renew my desire to forge ahead. God does not make our wilderness. He is there with us trying to make us move ahead.' I do not think I could find a better expression of the living praxis which young people can teach us to resume. I wanted to show by means of four inseparable prophetic forces that young people are an inspiration for the present-day world.

Note

The limits of this article do not allow me to explain at length the actual consequences of this prophetic paradigm offered by the challenge and drama of young people. Nevertheless, I should like to draw attention to a social and pastoral praxis which seems of primary importance in the present crisis. We must remember first that the situation of young people in the present crisis is very different from that which the young people's movements experienced in the 1960s when, almost everywhere in the world, young people asked for radical changes to be made, but within the framework of a world which thought it was committed to irreversible progress. Instead the present-day context is one where almost all sectors, apart from technological innovation, are blocked simultaneously. In such circumstances young people turn first to cultural practices to express their discontent, experience and aspirations. They use these cultural phenomena to manufacture a 'meaning', 'community' and 'workplace'. In pastoral and theological terms, this cultural praxis may be seen as a 'sacramental' process. Young people invent signs, secular liturgies which try to name and signify something at a deep feeling-level which has not yet found any actual social or ecclesial form. The term 'expression' already reflects this initial form of practice: 'ex-expression': that is, to let the pressure out, but also what is lived, felt, intuited and dreamed. The generations of codification and writing tried to give formal expression to contents. The present generation prefers to use expressive cultural means to conceive, produce and share new contents. For the moment, young people are trying to name and signify the four prophetic forces which I have just analysed. They feel, intuit and project them—above all in cultural forms which precede their social, political or economic actions.

It is also interesting to note that these cultural expressions are to be found in tendencies of the alternative society (pacifism, ecology, and so on), contrary to the 1960s when the youth phenomenon was located mainly in an exclusive subculture. This is probably the sign of a process of political maturation which all those inquiries into youth have not discerned, since almost all of them have reached the conclusion of a so-called 'de-politicisation' of young people. That seems to be the case only in the context of our own political and ideological codes. Young people are bearers not only of new goals but of new ways of reaching them. In their cultural-sacramental pursuits we can discern both their new forms of practice and the prophetic paradigm which I have discussed in this article. Social or pastoral intervention by adults has to change its ways of looking, thinking and acting!

Translated by J. G. Cumming

Contributors

EILEEN BARKER is currently the Dean of Undergraduate Studies at the London School of Economics, where she has been a member of the department of sociology since 1970. Her research has been mainly in the sociology of religion, particularly the new religious movements and the relationship between science and religion in contemporary society. She is the author of *The Making of a Moonie: Brainwashing or Choice?* (1984), the editor of *Of Gods and Men: New Religious Movements in the West* (1984) and *New Religious Movements: A Perspective for Understanding Society* (1982), and has contributed over sixty articles to various books and journals. Dr Barker is on the Executive Council of the Society for the Scientific Study of Religion and the Conférence Internationale de Sociologie des Religions.

ANS JOACHIM VAN DER BENT has been the Librarian of the World Council of Churches since 1963. He is a citizen of the Netherlands and an ordained minister in the United Church of Christ (USA). He has written several books, produced various reference works, and contributed over fifty articles to theological journals. His latest book is entitled: *Incarnation and New Creation—The Ecumenical Movement at the Cross Roads*, published by the Christian Literature Society in Madras.

JACQUES GRAND'MAISON was born in 1931. After doctorates in sociology and theology, he became professor with a personal chair at the University of Montréal, Canada, where he has taught since 1965. For more than twenty years he has been concerned with social and pastoral projects for regional development, educational reform, urban renewal, workers' movements, and overall pastoral strategy. His experiences of the recycling of the young unemployed inspired new Canadian social policies in this area. He has also taken part in self-help projects in Europe and Africa. Among his most recent publications are: *Quel homme? Quelle société* (1978), *Au seuil critique d'un nouvel âge* (1979), *La nouvelle classe* (1980), *Une Foi ensouchée dans ce pays* (1980), *De quel droit?* 2 vols (1981), *La Révolution affective* (1983).

BARBARA HARGROVE is Professor of the Sociology of Religion at the Iliff School of Theology in Denver, Colorado. She has taught at Hollins College in Virginia, The University of North Florida in Jacksonville, and the Yale Divinity School, as well as spending a year working with the 'new religious consciousness' team at the University of California in Berkeley. She is currently Vice President of the Association for the Sociology of Religion, and has served as President of the Religious Research Association and on the Council of the Society for the Scientific Study of Religion. Among her publications are *Sociology of Religion: Classic and Contemporary Approaches* (1979), *Religion for a Dislocated Generation* (1980), and *Women of the Cloth*, with Jackson Carroll and Adair Lummis (1983), as well as a number of book chapters and journal articles and an edited book, *Religion and the Sociology of Knowledge* (1984).

AL HATTON is currently National Director of the YMCA Job Generation programme for the National Council of YMCAs of Canada. He was formerly Executive Director of the Downtown Montreal YMCA and in the early seventies was working with alienated youth. In recent years, he has been involved with a number of movements and projects touching on issues of urban renewal, transportation, environment, services for seniors and coalition building.

PAUL KAPTEYN was born in 1942 and studied theology and sociology in Amsterdam. He graduated in 1980 with his dissertation 'Taboe, ontwikkelingen in macht en moraal, speciaal in Nederland' (Amsterdam 1980) and is at present working on a book on the relationship between older and younger people, provisionally entitled *In the Recreation Ground of the Netherlands*. He is a member of the professional group known as 'Sociology and History' at the University of Amsterdam.

KEES KWANT took his degree in scholastic philosophy at the Angelicum in Rome in 1945 and studied subsequently at the Sorbonne in Paris and at Louvain. He is concerned with phenomenological and structuralist philosophy, and his most prominent field of study is social philosophy and his speciality the philosophy of work. Among his works in this field is *Het arbeidsbestel: een studie over de geest van onze samenleving* (1956), which was the first to use the term *arbeidsbestel* (translated here as 'world of work') that quickly came into general usage. Other works include: *De ontmoeting van wetenschap en arbeid* (1958); *Philosophy of Labor* (1960); *Filosofie van de arbeid* (1964); and *Werkloosheid als uitdaging* (1983).

RENÉ LAURENTIN was born in 1917 and ordained priest in 1946. He holds doctorates from the Sorbonne and the Institut Catholique de Paris, and teaches theology at the University of the West (in Angers), having previously lectured at universities in Canada, the USA and Latin America. He was an adviser to the preparatory theological commission for Vatican II and then a *peritus* at the Council. Many of his sixty published works have dealt with Mary, pilgrimages, Vatican II and synods; among those translated into English: *Mary's Place in the Church* (1966).

JÜAN ANDRÉS PERETIATKOWICZ is a member of the Congregation of the Sacred Hearts and was ordained in 1963. He studied Psychology and Pedagogy at the Institut Catholique in Paris, and the theology of the religious life in Madrid, from 1968–72. Since 1982 he has worked as episcopal delegate for the pastoral care of young people in the Archdiocese of Santiago.

MIKLÓS TOMKA was born in Budapest in 1941. After gaining doctorates in sociology he did research into communications and minorities. He researches and teaches sociology of religion. Since 1978 he has been vice-president of the sociology of religion section of the International Sociological Association. In addition to works in Hungarian, he has published in (among others) *Social Compass, Lumen Vitae, The Annual Review of the Social Sciences of Religion, Probleme des Friedens, Nauka i Religia.*

MICHAEL WARREN received his doctorate in religious education from the Catholic University of America in 1974. Since 1975, he has taught in the Theology Department at St John's University, New York City, where he is currently professor for religious education and catechetical ministry. He has lectured in Canada, Ireland, New Zealand and Australia. In 1982, he and a group of eight others helped start The Youth for Peace Project, whose aim is to give young people a way of speaking on issues of peace and social justice. His recent books are: *Youth and the Future of the Church* (1982) and *The Sourcebook for Modern Catechetics* (1983).

CONCILIUM

1. (Vol. 1 No. 1) **Dogma.** Ed. Edward Schillebeeckx. 86pp.
2. (Vol. 2 No. 1) **Liturgy.** Ed. Johannes Wagner. 100pp.
3. (Vol. 3 No. 1) **Pastoral.** Ed. Karl Rahner. 104pp.
4. (Vol. 4 No. 1) **Ecumenism.** Hans Küng. 108pp.
5. (Vol. 5 No. 1) **Moral Theology.** Ed. Franz Bockle. 98pp.
6. (Vol. 6 No. 1) **Church and World.** Ed. Johannes Baptist Metz. 92pp.
7. (Vol. 7 No. 1) **Church History.** Roger Aubert. 92pp.
8. (Vol. 8 No. 1) **Canon Law.** Ed. Teodoro Jimenez Urresti and Neophytos Edelby. 96pp.
9. (Vol. 9 No. 1) **Spirituality.** Ed. Christian Duquoc. 88pp.
10. (Vol. 10 No. 1) **Scripture.** Ed. Pierre Benoit and Roland Murphy. 92pp.
11. (Vol. 1 No. 2) **Dogma.** Ed. Edward Shillebeeckx. 88pp.
12. (Vol. 2 No. 2) **Liturgy.** Ed. Johannes Wagner. 88pp.
13. (Vol. 3 No. 2) **Pastoral.** Ed. Karl Rahner. 84pp.
14. (Vol. 4 No. 2) **Ecumenism.** Ed. Hans Küng. 96pp.
15. (Vol. 5 No. 2) **Moral Theology.** Ed. Franz Bockle. 88pp.
16. (Vol. 6 No. 2) **Church and World.** Ed. Johannes Baptist Metz. 84pp.
17. (Vol. 7 No. 2) **Church History.** Ed. Roger Aubert. 96pp.
18. (Vol. 8 No. 2) **Religious Freedom.** Ed. Neophytos Edelby and Teodoro Jimenez Urresti. 96pp.
19. (Vol. 9 No. 2) **Religionless Christianity?** Ed. Christian Duquoc. 96pp.
20. (Vol. 10 No. 2) **The Bible and Tradition.** Ed. Pierre Benoit and Roland E. Murphy. 96pp.
21. (Vol. 1 No. 3) **Revelation and Dogma.** Ed. Edward Schillebeeckx. 88pp.
22. (Vol. 2 No. 3) **Adult Baptism and Initiation.** Ed. Johannes Wagner. 96pp.
23. (Vol. 3 No. 3) **Atheism and Indifference.** Ed. Karl Rahner. 92pp.
24. (Vol. 4 No. 3) **The Debate on the Sacraments.** Ed. Hans Küng. 92pp.
25. (Vol. 5 No. 3) **Morality, Progress and History.** Ed. Franz Bockle. 84pp.
26. (Vol. 6 No. 3) **Evolution.** Ed. Johannes Baptist Metz. 88pp.
27. (Vol. 7 No. 3) **Church History.** Ed. Roger Aubert. 92pp.
28. (Vol. 8 No. 3) **Canon Law—Theology and Renewal.** Ed. Neophytos Edelby and Teodoro Jimenez Urresti. 92pp.
29. (Vol. 9 No. 3) **Spirituality and Politics.** Ed. Christian Duquoc. 84pp.
30. (Vol. 10 No. 3) **The Value of the Old Testament.** Ed. Pierre Benoit and Roland Murphy. 92pp.
31. (Vol. 1 No. 4) **Man, World and Sacrament.** Ed. Edward Schillebeeckx. 84pp.
32. (Vol. 2 No. 4) **Death and Burial: Theology and Liturgy.** Ed. Johannes Wagner. 88pp.

33. (Vol. 3 No. 4) **Preaching the Word of God.** Ed. Karl Rahner. 96pp.
34. (Vol. 4 No. 4) **Apostolic by Succession?** Ed. Hans Küng. 96pp.
35. (Vol. 5 No. 4) **The Church and Social Morality.** Ed. Franz Bockle. 92pp.
36. (Vol. 6 No. 4) **Faith and the World of Politics.** Ed. Johannes Baptist Metz. 96pp.
37. (Vol. 7 No. 4) **Prophecy.** Ed. Roger Aubert. 80pp.
38. (Vol. 8 No. 4) **Order and the Sacraments.** Ed. Neophytos Edelby and Teodoro Jimenez Urresti. 96pp.
39. (Vol. 9 No. 4) **Christian Life and Eschatology.** Ed. Christian Duquoc. 94pp.
40. (Vol. 10 No. 4) **The Eucharist: Celebrating the Presence of the Lord.** Ed. Pierre Benoit and Roland Murphy. 88pp.
41. (Vol. 1 No. 5) **Dogma.** Ed. Edward Schillebeeckx. 84pp.
42. (Vol. 2 No. 5) **The Future of Liturgy.** Ed. Johannes Wagner. 92pp.
43. (Vol. 3 No. 5) **The Ministry and Life of Priests Today.** Ed. Karl Rahner. 104pp.
44. (Vol. 4 No. 5) **Courage Needed.** Ed. Hans Küng. 92pp.
45. (Vol. 5 No. 5) **Profession and Responsibility in Society.** Ed. Franz Bockle. 84pp.
46. (Vol. 6 No. 5) **Fundamental Theology.** Ed. Johannes Baptist Metz. 84pp.
47. (Vol. 7 No. 5) **Sacralization in the History of the Church.** Ed. Roger Aubert. 80pp.
48. (Vol. 8 No. 5) **The Dynamism of Canon Law.** Ed. Neophytos Edelby and Teodoro Jimenez Urresti. 92pp.
49. (Vol. 9 No. 5) **An Anxious Society Looks to the Gospel.** Ed. Christian Duquoc. 80pp.
50. (Vol. 10 No. 5) **The Presence and Absence of God.** Ed. Pierre Benoit and Roland Murphy. 88pp.
51. (Vol. 1 No. 6) **Tension between Church and Faith.** Ed. Edward Schillebeeckx. 160pp.
52. (Vol. 2 No. 6) **Prayer and Community.** Ed. Herman Schmidt. 156pp.
53. (Vol. 3 No. 6) **Catechetics for the Future.** Ed. Alois Müller. 168pp.
54. (Vol. 4 No. 6) **Post-Ecumenical Christianity.** Ed. Hans Küng. 168pp.
55. (Vol. 5 No. 6) **The Future of Marriage as Institution.** Ed. Franz Bockle. 180pp.
56. (Vol. 6 No. 6) **Moral Evil Under Challenge.** Ed. Johannes Baptist Metz. 160pp.
57. (Vol. 7 No. 6) **Church History at a Turning Point.** Ed. Roger Aubert. 160pp.
58. (Vol. 8 No. 6) **Structures of the Church's Presence in the World of Today.** Ed. Teodoro Jimenez Urresti. 160pp.
59. (Vol. 9 No. 6) **Hope.** Ed. Christian Duquoc. 160pp.
60. (Vol. 10 No. 6) **Immortality and Resurrection.** Ed. Pierre Benoit and Roland Murphy. 160pp.

61. (Vol. 1 No. 7) **The Sacramental Administration of Reconciliation** Ed. Edward Schillebeeckx. 160p
62. (Vol. 2 No. 7) **Worship of Christian Man Today.** Ed. Herman Schmidt. 156pp.
63. (Vol. 3 No. 7) **Democratization the Church.** Ed. Alois Müller. 160pp.
64. (Vol. 4 No. 7) **The Petrine Ministry in the Church.** Ed. Han Küng. 160pp.
65. (Vol. 5 No. 7) **The Manipulatio of Man.** Ed. Franz Bockle. 144p
66. (Vol. 6 No. 7) **Fundamental Theology in the Church.** Ed. Johannes Baptist Metz. 156pp.
67. (Vol. 7 No. 7) **The Self-Understanding of the Church.** E Roger Aubert. 144pp.
68. (Vol. 8 No. 7) **Contestation in** Church. Ed. Teodoro Jimenez Urresti. 152pp.
69. (Vol. 9 No. 7) **Spirituality, Pub or Private?** Ed. Christian Duqu 156pp.
70. (Vol. 10 No. 7) **Theology, Exegesis and Proclamation.** Ed. Roland Murphy. 144pp.
71. (Vol. 1 No. 8) **The Bishop and Unity of the Church.** Ed. Edwa Schillebeeckx. 156pp.
72. (Vol. 2 No. 8) **Liturgy and the Ministry.** Ed. Herman Schmidt 160pp.
73. (Vol. 3 No. 8) **Reform of the Church.** Ed. Alois Müller and Norbert Greinacher. 152pp.
74. (Vol. 4 No. 8) **Mutual Recogni of Ecclesial Ministries?** Ed. Ha Küng and Walter Kasper. 152
75. (Vol. 5 No. 8) **Man in a New Society.** Ed. Franz Bockle. 16C
76. (Vol. 6 No. 8) **The God Questi** Ed. Johannes Baptist Metz. 156pp.
77. (Vol. 7 No. 8) **Election-Consen Reception.** Ed. Giuseppe Albe and Anton Weiler. 156pp.
78. (Vol. 8 No. 8) **Celibacy of the Catholic Priest.** Ed. William Bassett and Peter Huizing. 16C
79. (Vol. 9 No. 8) **Prayer.** Ed. Christian Duquoc and Claude Geffré. 126pp.
80. (Vol. 10 No. 8) **Ministries in t** Church. Ed. Bas van Iersel an Roland Murphy. 152pp.
81. **The Persistence of Religion.** E Andrew Greeley and Gregory Baum. 0 8164 2537 X 168pp.
82. **Liturgical Experience of Faith.** Herman Schmidt and David Power. 0 8164 2538 8 144pp.
83. **Truth and Certainty.** Ed. Edw Schillebeeckx and Bas van Ier 0 8164 2539 6 144pp.
84. **Political Commitment and Christian Community.** Ed. Alc Müller and Norbert Greinach 0 8164 2540 X 156pp.
85. **The Crisis of Religious Langu** Ed. Johannes Baptist Metz ar Jean-Pierre Jossua. 0 8164 254 144pp.
86. **Humanism and Christianity.** E Claude Geffré. 0 8164 2542 6 144pp.
87. **The Future of Christian Marr** Ed. William Bassett and Pete Huizing. 0 8164 2575 2.

3. **Polarization in the Church.** Ed. Hans Küng and Walter Kasper. 0 8164 2572 8 156pp.
). **Spiritual Revivals.** Ed. Christian Duquoc and Casiano Floristán. 0 8164 2573 6 156pp.
). **Power and the Word of God.** Ed. Franz Bockle and Jacques Marie Pohier. 0 8164 2574 4 156pp.
. **The Church as Institution.** Ed. Gregory Baum and Andrew Greeley. 0 8164 2575 2 168pp.
. **Politics and Liturgy.** Ed. Herman Schmidt and David Power. 0 8164 2576 0 156pp.
. **Jesus Christ and Human Freedom.** Ed. Edward Schillebeeckx and Bas van Iersel. 0 8164 2577 9 168pp.
. **The Experience of Dying.** Ed. Norbert Greinacher and Alois Müller. 0 8164 2578 7 156pp.
. **Theology of Joy.** Ed. Johannes Baptist Metz and Jean-Pierre Jossua. 0 8164 2579 5 164pp.
. **The Mystical and Political Dimension of the Christian Faith.** Ed. Claude Geffré and Gustavo Guttierez. 0 8164 2580 9 168pp.
. **The Future of the Religious Life.** Ed. Peter Huizing and William Bassett. 0 8164 2094 7 96pp.
. **Christians and Jews.** Ed. Hans Küng and Walter Kasper. 0 8164 2095 5 96pp.
Experience of the Spirit. Ed. Peter Huizing and William Bassett. 0 8164 2096 3 144pp.
Sexuality in Contemporary Catholicism. Ed. Franz Bockle and Jacques Marie Pohier. 0 8164 2097 1 126pp.
Ethnicity. Ed. Andrew Greeley and Gregory Baum. 0 8164 2145 5 120pp.
Liturgy and Cultural Religious Traditions. Ed. Herman Schmidt and David Power. 0 8164 2146 2 120pp.
A Personal God? Ed. Edward Schillebeeckx and Bas van Iersel. 0 8164 2149 8 142pp.
The Poor and the Church. Ed. Norbert Greinacher and Alois Müller. 0 8164 2147 1 128pp.
Christianity and Socialism. Ed. Johannes Baptist Metz and Jean-Pierre Jossua. 0 8164 2148 X 144pp.
The Churches of Africa: Future Prospects. Ed. Claude Geffré and Bertrand Luneau. 0 8164 2150 1 128pp.
Judgement in the Church. Ed. William Bassett and Peter Huizing. 0 8164 2166 8 128pp.
Why Did God Make Me? Ed. Hans Küng and Jürgen Moltmann. 0 8164 2167 6 112pp.
Charisms in the Church. Ed. Christian Duquoc and Casiano Floristán. 0 8164 2168 4 128pp.
Moral Formation and Christianity. Ed. Franz Bockle and Jacques Marie Pohier. 0 8164 2169 2 120pp.
Communication in the Church. Ed. Gregory Baum and Andrew Greeley. 0 8164 2170 6 126pp.

112. **Liturgy and Human Passage.** Ed. David Power and Luis Maldonado. 0 8164 2608 2 136pp.
113. **Revelation and Experience.** Ed. Edward Schillebeeckx and Bas van Iersel. 0 8164 2609 0 134pp.
114. **Evangelization in the World Today.** Ed. Norbert Greinacher and Alois Müller. 0 8164 2610 4 136pp.
115. **Doing Theology in New Places.** Ed. Jean-Pierre Jossua and Johannes Baptist Metz. 0 8164 2611 2 120pp.
116. **Buddhism and Christianity.** Ed. Claude Geffré and Mariasusai Dhavamony. 0 8164 2612 0 136pp.
117. **The Finances of the Church.** Ed. William Bassett and Peter Huizing. 0 8164 2197 8 160pp.
118. **An Ecumenical Confession of Faith?** Ed. Hans Küng and Jürgen Moltmann. 0 8164 2198 6 136pp.
119. **Discernment of the Spirit and of Spirits.** Ed. Casiano Floristán and Christian Duquoc. 0 8164 2199 4 136pp.
120. **The Death Penalty and Torture.** Ed. Franz Bockle and Jacques Marie Pohier. 0 8164 2200 1 136pp.
121. **The Family in Crisis or in Transition.** Ed. Andrew Greeley. 0 567 30001 3 128pp.
122. **Structures of Initiation in Crisis.** Ed. Luis Maldonado and David Power. 0 567 30002 1 128pp.
123. **Heaven.** Ed. Bas van Iersel and Edward Schillebeeckx. 0 567 30003 X 120pp.
124. **The Church and the Rights of Man.** Ed. Alois Müller and Norbert Greinacher. 0 567 30004 8 140pp.
125. **Christianity and the Bourgeoisie.** Ed. Johannes Baptist Metz. 0 567 30005 6 144pp.
126. **China as a Challenge to the Church.** Ed. Claude Geffré and Joseph Spae. 0 567 30006 4 136pp.
127. **The Roman Curia and the Communion of Churches.** Ed. Peter Huizing and Knut Walf. 0 567 30007 2 144pp.
128. **Conflicts about the Holy Spirit.** Ed. Hans Küng and Jürgen Moltmann. 0 567 30008 0 144pp.
129. **Models of Holiness.** Ed. Christian Duquoc and Casiano Floristán. 0 567 30009 9 128pp.
130. **The Dignity of the Despised of the Earth.** Ed. Jacques Marie Pohier and Dietmar Mieth. 0 567 30010 2 144pp.
131. **Work and Religion.** Ed. Gregory Baum. 0 567 30011 0 148pp.
132. **Symbol and Art in Worship.** Ed. Luis Maldonado and David Power. 0 567 30012 9 136pp.
133. **Right of the Community to a Priest.** Ed. Edward Schillebeeckx and Johannes Baptist Metz. 0 567 30013 7 148pp.
134. **Women in a Men's Church.** Ed. Virgil Elizondo and Norbert Greinacher. 0 567 30014 5 144pp.
135. **True and False Universality of Christianity.** Ed. Claude Geffré and Jean-Pierre Jossua. 0 567 30015 3 138pp.

136. **What is Religion? An Inquiry for Christian Theology.** Ed. Mircea Eliade and David Tracy. 0 567 30016 1 98pp.
137. **Electing our Own Bishops.** Ed. Peter Huizing and Knut Walf. 0 567 30017 X 112pp.
138. **Conflicting Ways of Interpreting the Bible.** Ed. Hans Küng and Jürgen Moltmann. 0 567 30018 8 112pp.
139. **Christian Obedience.** Ed. Casiano Floristán and Christian Duquoc. 0 567 30019 6 96pp.
140. **Christian Ethics and Economics: the North-South Conflict.** Ed. Dietmar Mieth and Jacques Marie Pohier. 0 567 30020 X 128pp.
141. **Neo-Conservatism: Social and Religious Phenomenon.** Ed. Gregory Baum and John Coleman. 0 567 30021 8.
142. **The Times of Celebration.** Ed. David Power and Mary Collins. 0 567 30022 6.
143. **God as Father.** Ed. Edward Schillebeeckx and Johannes Baptist Metz. 0 567 30023 4.
144. **Tensions Between the Churches of the First World and the Third World.** Ed. Virgil Elizondo and Norbert Greinacher. 0 567 30024 2.
145. **Nietzsche and Christianity.** Ed. Claude Geffré and Jean-Pierre Jossua. 0 567 30025 0.
146. **Where Does the Church Stand?** Ed. Giuseppe Alberigo. 0 567 30026 9.
147. **The Revised Code of Canon Law: a Missed Opportunity?** Ed. Peter Huizing and Knut Walf. 0 567 30027 7.
148. **Who Has the Say in the Church?** Ed. Hans Küng and Jürgen Moltmann. 0 567 30028 5.
149. **Francis of Assisi Today.** Ed. Casiano Floristán and Christian Duquoc. 0 567 30029 3.
150. **Christian Ethics: Uniformity, Universality, Pluralism.** Ed. Jacques Pohier and Dietmar Mieth. 0 567 30030 7.
151. **The Church and Racism.** Ed. Gregory Baum and John Coleman. 0 567 30031 5.
152. **Can we always celebrate the Eucharist?** Ed. Mary Collins and David Power. 0 567 30032 3.
153. **Jesus, Son of God?** Ed. Edward Schillebeeckx and Johannes-Baptist Metz. 0 567 30033 1.
154. **Religion and Churches in Eastern Europe.** Ed. Virgil ELizondo and Norbert Greinacher. 0 567 30034 X.
155. **'The Human', Criterion of Christian Existence?** Ed. Claude Geffré and Jean-Pierre Jossua. 0 567 30035 8.
156. **The Challenge of Psychology to Faith.** Ed. Steven Kepnes (Guest Editor) and David Tracy. 0 567 30036 6.
157. **May Church Ministers be Politicians?** Ed. Peter Huizing and Knut Walf. 0 567 30037 4.
158. **The Right to Dissent.** Ed. Hans Küng and Jürgen Moltmann. 0 567 30038 2.

CONCILIUM

159. **Learning to Pray.** Ed. Casiano
     Floristán and Christian Duquoc.
     0 567 30039 0.
160. **Unemployment and the Right to
     Work.** Ed. Dietmar Mieth and
     Jacques Pohier. 0 567 30040 4.
161. **New Religious Movements.** Ed. by
     John Coleman and Gregory
     Baum.
162. **Liturgy: A Creative Tradition.** Ed.
     by Mary Collins and David
     Power.

163. **Martyrdom Today.** Ed. by
     Johannes-Baptist Metz and
     Edward Schillebeeckx.
164. **Church and Peace.** Ed. by Virgil
     Elizondo and Norbert Greinacher.
165. **Indifference to Religion.** Ed. by
     Claude Geffré and Jean-Pierre
     Jossua.
166. **Theology and Cosmology.** Ed. by
     David Tracy and Nicholas Lash.
167. **The Ecumenical Council and the
     Church Constitution.** Ed. by Peter
     Huizing and Knut Walf.

168. **Mary in the Churches.** Ed. by
     Hans Küng and Jürgen
     Moltmann.
169. **Job and the Silence of God.** Ed.
     by Christian Duquoc and Casiano
     Floristán.
170. **Twenty Years of Concilium—
     Retrospect and Prospect.** Ed. by
     Edward Schillebeeckx, Paul Brand
     and Anton Weiler.

CONCILIUM 1984

DIFFERENT THEOLOGIES, COMMON RESPONSIBILITY
Edited by Claude Geffre, Gustavo Gutierrez and Virgil
Elizondo   171

THE ETHICS OF LIBERATION—THE LIBERATION OF ETHICS
Edited by Dietmar Mieth and Jacques Pohier   172

THE SEXUAL REVOLUTION
Edited by Gregory Baum and John Coleman   173

THE TRANSMISSION OF FAITH TO THE NEXT GENERATION
Edited by Virgil Elizondo and Norbert Greinacher   174

THE HOLOCAUST AS INTERRUPTION
Edited by Elisabeth Fiorenza and David Tracy   175

LA IGLESIA POPULAR: BETWEEN FEAR AND HOPE
Edited by Leonardo Boff and Virgil Elizondo   176

*All back issues are still in print: available from bookshops (price £3.75)
or direct from the publisher (£4.25/US$7.45/Can$8.55 including postage
and packing).*

**T. & T. CLARK LTD, 36 GEORGE STREET,
EDINBURGH EH2 2LQ, SCOTLAND**

FEMINIST THEOLOGY

Next month in CONCILIUM

WOMEN-INVISIBLE IN CHURCH AND THEOLOGY

Edited by Elisabeth Schussler Fiorenza and Mary Collins

CONCILIUM looks at the whole nature of patriarchy in its practice and implications; and at the experience of women in theology, ecclesiastical structures, the liturgical proclemation of scripture, church history, ecumenism and Third World churches. There are case studies on women's theological education in Germany, North America and the Third World.

Issue 182   £3.75

Also available

WOMEN IN A MEN'S CHURCH

Edited by Virgil Elizondo and Norbert Greinacher

This reprinted issue of CONCILIUM examines the problems women face in theology both from a historical and contemporary perspective. The editors believe that it is only when men and women work together that the dominance of men can be undone and the freedom of women achieved in society and in the Church.

Issue 134   £3.75

CONCILIUM is available as single issues or by subscription

(*See backlist advertisement for current subscription rates*)

**T & T CLARK LTD, 59 GEORGE STREET,
EDINBURGH EH2 2LQ, SCOTLAND**